ISBN 979-8-9879290-3-2

Scriptural references pulled from:
Barrows, Cliff. *New King James Version Bible*. Thomas Nelson Produced by Christian Duplications International, 1983.

Written by Lance Crowe

Cover Artwork by Debarim Publishing

Published by
Debarim Publishing, LLC
807 W Broadway
Spiro, OK 74959
www.debarimpublishing.com

Disclaimer:

This book is designed to help the person dealing with suicidal thoughts, anyone dealing with an emotional crisis, and the people who want to understand and help.

Suicide is the last step in dealing with an emotional crisis. So even if you are not suicidal, you can benefit from the rest of the steps, maybe even preventing yourself from becoming suicidal, and then be able to help someone who is.

This book is not written by a licensed health professional, and is not intended to supersede medical advice. All information provided is solely from the author through life experiences and studying the Word. The views expressed in this book are not that of Debarim Publishing as Debarim Publishing makes no claims to medical knowledge regarding suicide or other topics discussed in this book.

If you feel the need or desire to commit suicide and are having trouble coping, call 911, 988, or the Suicide Hot-line to receive help.

National Suicide Prevention Hot-line
1-800-273-TALK 8255 or 1-800-SUICIDE 784-2433

This book is dedicate to Yahweh, the Father, the Son, and the Spirit. You gave me life and brought me to this season.

SUICIDE
SOBRIETY

By Lance Crowe

Table of Contents

Why Choose Sobriety

Why use the word "sobriety" when discussing suicide? Normally, "sobriety" is used for discussing alcohol or substance addictions, but we often forget that our thoughts can become addictive. When I was an adolescent boy, I remember having crushes on certain gals. Let me tell you, those thoughts, all by themselves, were quite addictive.

Negative thoughts are also addictive. Negative speech is addictive – think of people who are always gossiping, even after it ruins their relationships. Negative actions, like cutting, become addictive. Usually, when a person cuts themselves to deal with stress, they continue because the release provides the emotional and physiologic stimulus to continue cutting instead of finding a healthier way. The pain, both physical and emotional, from the cutting releases endorphins and gives the cutter some control over the other emotional pain they are experiencing. It can be done in private so as not to draw unwanted attention to themselves.

Let's be honest. It is difficult to know when a negative behavior is simply a pattern or an addiction because both can be challenging when replacing either with a healthy behavior and attitude. To me, the best three words for addiction are dependency, craving, and fixation. A pattern is a routine or habit without feelings of dependency, craving, or fixation.

Suicide is an Escape Mechanism

There are times in life when things happen that usually overload our emotional ability to cope. That is different for each person. Coping is dealing with the situation.

If you take a group of people who experience a traumatic event together, you will immediately notice different coping mechanisms being used or not used. Some will try to help, some will try to escape, and some will be nearly paralyzed. Later, you will see other changes. Some will talk about it and move on, others will pretend it never happened, and some will be profoundly changed by it on many different levels.

Painful events leave us all feeling vulnerable, and we all require a coping mechanism to help us return to a safe space. Whatever that mechanism is, it has to be greater than the pain or trauma. Otherwise, we will use something else to escape the pain. Escaping is not truly coping. Escaping is temporarily finding a safer space that is not safe. It is an in-between space.

Example: A woman takes her children out of the house where the man is physically abusing them. Since she does not know where to go, she drives them to a parking lot to sleep in the car until morning. Then, she can find something better that is safe, like a shelter for abused women and families.

The proper use of an escape mechanism is to use it until the coping mechanism is operating, which is very short-lived. The problem is that we encounter situations where we don't know what coping mechanism to use, and we get stuck in the escape mechanism. Using drugs and alcohol is very popular. Sadly, so is suicide. A coping mechanism brings us to a safe space that allows us to heal, move on, and help others. Staying in an escape mechanism prevents us from healing. If we can't heal, we can't move on and help others.

What is Suicide Sobriety?

While Chapter 2 discusses this question in length, the short answer is Suicide Sobriety is leaving the escape mechanism of suicide to enter into coping and healing to live a full life and help others.

Generally, We can say, sobriety is coping and living life and that addictions can be anything you are dependent on that interferes with coping and living life. One of the best coping mechanisms is simply asking for help until you get it. Praying is the best way to ask for help.

Suicide has Physical, Mental, and Spiritual Components

Contemplating suicide means that you have lost faith in whatever you previously relied on to cope. You have entered a phase in your crisis where you now have a genuine lack of trust in the things that you believed would safely get you through obstacles, so now, death appears to be your safe space.

The problem with life is that it shows us two things: either the things we have faith in are insufficient, or our faith is inadequate. Either way, we face the dilemma of what to put our trust in. What is trustworthy? Suicide is the illusion that death is trustworthy. The only thing that you can trust death with is death.

We can see someone use a process only to have that process fail for us because we did not understand it. This increases our tendency to distrust at a critical moment because we do not understand what went wrong, leading us to believe that self-destruction will fix what ails us.

As human beings, we are the most adept at dealing with problems in the physical and mental arenas because those are visible. Many, if not most, of our problems include an invisible spiritual component. Somehow, we feel the spiritual world around us, even if we don't understand it. Most people know that the spiritual world exists. However, most of the literature I reviewed when researching this book ignores this vital, life-giving fact. This means that most of what I read only dealt with the crisis phase in the body and mind.

To become truly sober from suicide or other emotional crises, there has to be a larger focus than simply looking at the crisis phase and how it affects the mind and body. Sobriety means becoming and staying healthy. A person's spirit must also be healthy and included in the overall suicide prevention matrix because a person's spirit, along with their mind and body, is affected by other spiritual entities. We are part of a much larger whole than the physical world.

The Spiritual World Consists of Life and Death

Some religions see this as a duality and try to live in harmony with it. Reality is more sobering. The spirits of death are in bitter opposition to the spirit of life. There is no duality. This is conflict, which spills over into our physical world. The oldest continually used and trusted religious text, the Bible, says, *"For we do not wrestle against flesh and blood, but against principalities, against powers, against the rulers of the darkness of this age, against spiritual hosts of wickedness in the heavenly places."* – Eph 6:12 NKJV.

The goal of the spiritual entities of darkness is your death. However, the spirit of life has placed boundaries on these spirits of death. The benefit is that they cannot kill you straight out. They need a human agent. If you don't kill yourself, they will try to find someone who will do it for them. Thankfully, the Yahweh knows when and how to work around death until it is our proper time if we are willing to live so long.

The Bible tells us that Yahweh (my best understanding of His name) created a beautiful and perfect world for us to inhabit. He gave us and His ministering angels in Heaven free will. However, we humans were given something more special than the angels: the use of free will to have friendship with Yahweh. In contradistinction, the angels have free will to serve Yahweh. We have two different reasons for existing.

Free will is interesting because it encapsulates logic, the ability to reason progressively and orderly, and emotion, which means understanding using feelings. Logic is the ability to identify an object. That object is a cup. Emotions are the feelings about the cup. That is my favorite cup. We use logic to determine a thing, while we use emotions to value it.

To understand suicide better, we have to ask the following question: Who are the spirits of darkness? They are the spirits of Yahweh. They embrace death – not theirs, but ours! The sad reason is that the only sure way to hurt Yahweh is to hurt what He loves. The giver of life is also the spirit of light.

Yahweh gave us His light, and then He imparted His life to us. Darkness hates Him and seeks to diminish His light and destroy His life. The only thing that darkness can give is death. It sounds simple. It is until we understand that darkness cannot kill us, or we will all be dead instantly. Humans do not have that limitation. For some reason, we have more ability to exercise our free will. This is probably because the earth we live on was given to us, and we were to exercise dominion over it, not them.

The Problem with Free Will

Free will is a two-edged sword, and we have to live with the consequences of which direction we go. First, Yahweh allowed us to choose life or death, blessing or cursing, good or evil. Second, Yahweh will enable us to accept the consequences, whether we like them or not. Third, choices have unintended consequences. We may not understand how daily decisions affect the world around us. Face it: You are constantly being affected—good and bad—by choices you never made. This makes life feel like chaos.

When life goes our way, we don't pay much attention to the chaos. When life turns against us, then we feel enveloped by turmoil. Yet, the chaos was always there. It was our perception that changed. This is why, one moment, you think suicide is for losers, and the next moment, you think it is your only way out of the chaos.

What went wrong?

Yahweh designed us to live in a world where we would experience love and satisfying life, a world where He would leave Heaven to be our friend for a part of each day. What we did not know is that before turning this place into a paradise for us to live in, Yahweh expelled the angels He created to serve Him, those who used their free will to rebel against him, down here. Why? I think it's because love isn't love until it has survived a choice. Can you honestly say you love someone if that person was the only person you knew?

We were given the same choice as the angels in Heaven: Yahweh or Lucifer, life or death. Lucifer was Yahweh's greatest creation in Heaven. However, while Lucifer served Yahweh on His throne, he wanted to sit on that throne and receive the praises that were his job to give Yahweh.

All of the problems we face down here stem from that dissatisfaction. Lucifer took his dissatisfaction to some of the angels. After losing the rebellion, Lucifer was exiled here and already spread that same dissatisfaction. So where does that leave us? Unlike the angels, we have the ultimate choice. We are given the ability to decide.

The prophet Moshe codified this ultimate choice in his book: *I call heaven and earth as witnesses today against you, that I have set before you life and death, blessing and cursing; therefore choose life, that both you and your descendants may live; that you may love the Lord your God, that you may obey His voice, and that you may cling to Him, for He is your life and the length of your days...* Deut 30:19-20a NKJV.

Notice that we are encouraged to choose life but are not forced to. Yahweh is a gentleman. It's our choice—that is free will. We are given that gift to choose for ourselves—not for others. Our choices affect others. When we choose life, we bless others. When we choose death, we curse others.

So why don't we just "Choose life?"

That seems perfectly logical, right? The problem is that logic and emotions cannot fill the same mental space. You have to choose to think logically or emotionally and choose what to focus on, whether logical or emotional.

The darkness is going to make a compelling case for death. "Really, Lance! There's a compelling case for death?" you ask incredulously. "Yes," I say, "Sadly, but yes."

We discover that Lucifer comes to the first two people Yahweh created after His presence is not with them. So, he goes behind Yahweh's back to talk to them. These two people, Adam and Eve, were placed not just anywhere on the good earth but in a special place Yahweh called the Garden of Eden. So, they had the best of the best.

In that garden, Yahweh planted two trees: one for Him, the Tree of Life, and one for Lucifer, the Tree of the Knowledge of good and evil, which we painfully discover is also the Tree of Death.

Disguised as a serpent, Lucifer does not have his first conversation about the Tree of Life. He is at the Tree that brings death. During this conversation, Eve expresses her concerns to Lucifer about the Tree of Knowledge of good and evil, not fully grasping how it is the Tree of Death. Examine how he appeals to her senses, primarily affecting her emotions, rather than appealing to her logic the way Yahweh did. *Then the serpent said to the woman, You will not surely die. For the God knows that in the day you eat of it your eyes will be opened, and you will be like God, knowing good and evil. – Gen 3:4-5 NKJV.*

Lucifer seems to make no mention of life. They only receive painful, disturbing knowledge that does not enhance life but destroys it. Notice how her emotions overcome their logic. Her logical mind knows that Yahweh said, *but of the tree of the knowledge of good and evil you shall not eat, for in the day that you eat of it you shall surely die. – Gen 2:17.* Her emotions grabbed the fruit of death because she was promised something that sounded much better than it was.

When Lucifer told Eve she would know the difference between good and evil, she had no idea the pain and despair that knowledge would bring. To know evil is to understand suffering and death. This was precisely what Yahweh earnestly desired to prevent. Lucifer conned them into committing suicide. Lucifer is still doing the same thing today, saying, "Death is freedom!" Death is not freedom. Life is freedom! Living means being free.

Lucifer only has Two Strategies when Dealing with us –

Everything Lucifer does is to cause premature death, but he's such a good con artist that he paints death up to look like life. We see its true nature only when we logically examine what he offers.

Prayer allows us to communicate with Yahweh, allowing Him to intervene by exposing the enemy's lies and offering His solutions to our problems. It takes faith to trust Yahweh and His solutions. Another part of faith is waiting for the right timing for His solutions. It is better to trust Yahweh than the one who would have us choose death.

There are two primary spirits Lucifer uses to convince people to end their lives. It begins with the spirit of criticism beating you down to help you open the door to the spirit of suicide. Criticism can be either internal or external, depending on your emotional state. Self-criticism is the best because it further plants the seeds of doubt and despair. However, a well-placed criticism from the right person at the right time can be devastating. The goal is doubt because it leads to despair.

Any doubt will do. Once doubt is in your head, it can kill just about anything. The job of the spirit of criticism is not to improve anything, as most people who use it think or hope. Its job is to tear down your mind and create doubt that leads to despair that causes you to sabotage whatever has meaning to you. After you lose meaning, it creates fear for your future. If you are fearful for your future, you lose hope. When you hit the loss of hope stage, the spirit of suicide offers a solution.

Our emotions can be hard enough to deal with alone, but to have a whisperer making it worse is a lot to deal with, even on a good day. I have had thoughts of suicide when I wasn't even thinking about it or had a reason to. When I stopped to think about where it came from, I could quickly change my mind without real distress or lingering doubt. That is when I knew it was an entity.

Hope allows us to move forward when experiencing the worst of problems. Hope is what gets us through things daily, more than we think it does. Hopelessness is the key to bringing our life to a screeching halt. It takes away our drive to go after a life worth living. It can crush us with doubt about a better future.

The Two Things Lucifer Always Attacks

Since Lucifer is brilliant, he only has to focus on two core things. He can manipulate us in various ways from those two deep internal parts of our being. He attacks our core values and our core identity. What I find fascinating is that he does not attack our identity first, and I have often wondered why. By attacking something that comes from the external aspect of ourselves, he can open the door to the deeper aspect of our person. If he first struck at our identity, we would be instantly guarded, and that defense would likely prevent him from taking down our values.

Values are the how of what we believe. It's how we believe things should work, especially in behavior. Our behavior is based entirely on our values. Changing our values changes our behavior.

Our identity is who we truly believe we are, regardless of external behavior or outside conditions. We protect the part of us the most because we view ourselves through this lens.

Here is something to remember: all advertising aims to create new values and identity. It gets worse: virtually everything you see in the news, TV shows, movies, plays, social media, etc, is specifically designed to recreate your values and identity. So, if you feel inadequate, you may be watching too much of this world's propaganda. Your mental health may need a break from the news, especially entertainment and social media.

What Yahweh wants for you

For I know the thoughts that I think toward you, says the Lord, thoughts of peace and not of evil, to give you a future and a hope. – Jer 29:11 NKJV. *And we know that all things work together for good to those who love God, to those who are the called according to His purpose.* – Rom 8:28 NKJV.

The Word of Yahweh is sharper than a two-edged sword against the spirits of death. The two verses above can be taken and personalized to help you rebuild hope. Write out the two verses that are personalized to you. You should take an index card and write them down. Then, read them several times a day. *Death and life are in the power of the tongue, and those who love it will eat its fruit. - Prov 18:21*

You get to choose which fruit to eat. This gives you power over your circumstances and helps you control your own emotions. When death looks so appealing, we must find what is more attractive to leave that darkness behind. As Messiah said in John 10:10b NKJV, *"I have come that they may have life and that they may have it more abundantly."*

Prayer:

"Dear Father Yahweh, I'm trusting You now to give me hope to live one more day. You have a better life for me than I do now. Please give me Your spirit of life to fight against this spirit of death. In Yahushua (Jesus) name, amein."

What is Sobriety

Sobriety is not what I thought it was when I was given the thought that the way to cope with suicidal temptation was to be sober from suicide literally. This thought was not my own. Yahweh inspired me, and it also helped me focus on a solution rather than the problem, which is the key to sobriety in general.

Growing up around folks who attended A.A. (Alcoholics Anonymous), I understood that sobriety was complete abstinence from whatever it was that one wanted to be sober from. However, like many things, it is much more nuanced than that. Once I understood the nuances of sobriety, I began to understand why that particular word instead of abstinence, avoidance, or even celibacy. Just kidding about celibacy. It would be a catchy title – Suicide Celibacy.

Sobriety from Merriam-Webster, selected entries:
1. Marked by sedate or gravely or earnestly thoughtful character or demeanor.
2. Unhurried, calm.
3. Showing no excessive or extreme qualities of fancy, emotion, or prejudice.

As you can see, abstinence is not the concept of sobriety. However, one could make the case that it could lead one in that direction. Honestly, I don't know how one can ever be completely abstinent from having suicidal thoughts. Yet, I do hope, as you do, for complete abstinence from committing suicide.

As I began to think about the real meaning of sobriety, I realized how important it is to have "calm" amid the emotional storm that leads to suicide. Yahweh can bring us that calm when we ask for it and take those deep, calming breaths as He begins His work of bringing calm to the storm raging inside our head. The storms will always come, but our choice is how we react to them. This means that sobriety is not having an excessive emotional reaction, no matter how tempting it is to have one. Rather, be thoughtful while earnestly finding another solution.

Wanting to die is not natural. So, when we open the door to suicidal ideation, it will open again and again. We must find a way to keep closing the door every time it opens. As I mentioned before, sometimes the door opens from the outside when we're not even thinking about it.

We know that suicide is not our first option for dealing with crises or other serious stressors. Therefore, we can take the option of committing suicide off of the table. By taking it off the table, we can be confident that we will find another solution elsewhere. Which also gives us more confidence that a better solution will always be found. That gives us the patience to wait for it to come to us. While that may sound easier than it is, that's how it has to work. We have to make suicide a non-option. How do we take suicide off the table?

First, we need to recognize that we still have other options, some of which we probably have successfully used before, like talking to someone we trust, journaling, praying, exercising, and even taking time out. Praying, in my experience, is always the best place to start because Yahweh can direct us to the option that is best for us at this moment.

Second, we want to avoid using harmful escape mechanisms, like alcohol, drugs, inappropriate sex, outbursts of rage, overeating, breaking valuables, or running away. We don't want to increase our feelings of regret. Regret will put us back in a cycle of potential self-harm.

Vicious Cycle of Self-Harm

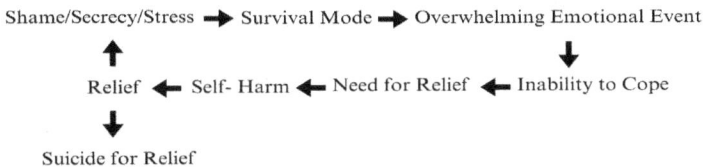

Shame/Secrecy/Stress ➡ Survival Mode ➡ Overwhelming Emotional Event

⬆   ⬇

Relief ⬅ Self- Harm ⬅ Need for Relief ⬅ Inability to Cope

⬇

Suicide for Relief

Emotional sobriety is dealing with the self-harm cycle in the same/secrecy/ stress and overwhelming emotional event phases before devolving into the inability to cope phase, and possibly eliminate "survival mode" altogether. However, it is still possible to stop yourself from self-harming if you can reach out for help or just stop yourself long enough to pause, take a deep breath, and think about your options.

We are more at risk for self-harm if we are dealing with a problem that brings us shame. This naturally causes us to be secretive; we are uncomfortable admitting it to others. It could be considered shameful or embarrassing, or we don't want to feel diminished in other people's eyes. Occasionally, we are involved in something that was not a problem until someone we looked up to turned it into one. We are stuck with the inability to deal with it because it is a shameful problem instead of a simple one.

Generally, we don't worry too much about simple problems. However, complex problems keep us up at night because we meditate on them, trying to see the problem and its potential solutions from many angles. Then, we play the "what if" game. What if this happens, or that happens, or this other thing happens? Our minds will get lost, and we feel hopeless.

When we are trying to solve more complex problems, it can be hard looking to other people outside our natural support group. This is due to natural distrust, but there can be safety in talking with someone who does not know you. They can be a little more open-minded and objective. Sometimes, it's just nice to have a listening ear.

A listening ear can break up the self-harm cycle because it ends the secrecy, which opens the door for dealing with stress. Without a listening ear, secrecy becomes a survival mechanism. Trust me, survival mode is very stressful when you can't break out of it. Survival Mode means that we can only deal with what is necessary to get by and little more. Life is no longer fun and seems to have no more purpose than simply to keep living. This makes us vulnerable to any event that now overwhelms us emotionally.

Imagine being unbalanced emotionally in survival mode. It doesn't take much to be tipped over, where we become emotionally overwhelmed. This is why it is so tough to cope with. Why? Because the emotional momentum picks up speed too quickly, we cannot cope. That leads to the desire for relief, and the quicker, the better. The quicker we want relief, the more likely we will make poor choices, worsening things.

This is where things can split. Depending on how often a person has been around this cycle or how severe it is at the beginning, the person may decide when to get off. So, the level of self-harm will depend on those factors, as the person chooses how severe the self-harm will need to be to gain relief.

Cycle of Self-Harm

Internal Emotional State

Down is a healthy emotional state where no self-harm will occur.

Low- Risk	Medium- Risk	High- Risk
↓	↓	↓
High emotional force to push into self-harm cycle	Medium emotional force to push into self-harm cycle	Low emotional force to push into self-harm cycle
↑	↑	↑

Emotional Resistance Pivot Point

Up is a unhealthy emotional state where self-harm is likely to occur.

When experiencing little to no shame/secrecy/stress, it takes the greatest emotional force to push our emotional state into the self-harm cycle. As the mass of shame/secrecy/stress increases in the person's internal emotional state, less emotional force is required to begin the cycle of self-harm. What raises the risk is a combination of duration – how long the person has dealt with the shame/secrecy/stress - and the severity of it – high intensity vs. low intensity. If the duration has been short, then the severity will need to be much worse to initiate self-harm for relief. Conversely, if the duration has been extended, then generally, the severity won't need to be very intense – the proverbial straw that broke the camel's back. Some people can experience a long duration and high severity before they finally tip over. Sadly, these people are often the most susceptible to suicide because when they snap, they snap hard.

The emotional resistance pivot point is not freewheeling. It has a certain amount of tension that prevents the emotional state from cycling. Naturally, it is different for each person. There are some other factors that can affect the strength of the pivot point, like H.A.L.T.S. This stands for hungry, angry, lonely, tired, and/or sick. It can include other physical or emotional factors that would never create a self-harm cycle. These weaken the pivot point.

Some people's pivot point is so strong that stress will only negatively affect them through long-term issues like weight gain, stress-related illness, relationship problems, drinking, smoking, partying, or not exercising. So, it makes the self-harm cycle look non-existent in the short term. It's more like long-term suicide, where it's very easy to deny there is a self-harm cycle. Yet, one actually exists because their behavior leads them to an early death.

Some escape mechanisms are self-harming, and yet we don't think of them as being suicidal. However, when a couple of guys on racing motorcycles are speeding down the freeway at up to twice the speed of the rest of the traffic, you instinctively realize that it is suicidal behavior. Notice that if one of them crashes and dies, their death will not be listed as "suicide" despite the obvious fact that they were engaging in self-harming behavior.

Sobriety Brings Calm to the Chaos

Chaos results when emotions are overwhelmed. The mind does not process effectively in this state. We use sobriety to prevent ourselves from going down the path of chaos.

Which looks something like this:

Chaos → Confusion → Acting Out → Regret → Hopelessness → Self-Destruction

The purpose of chaos is to create confusion, which prevents the mind from processing logically and finding a solution to the original problem. Instead, the mind acts out some maladaptive behavior that, when the chaotic moment passes, leaves us filled with feelings of regret for how we responded to the situation. Since we will have trouble coping now, we can slip into hopelessness, especially when someone points out our mistake, usually in a non-constructive and accusatory manner. To teach ourselves a lesson that we will not forget, we engage in self-destructive thoughts flowing into self-destructive words, eventually leading to self-harming behaviors.

A Navajo proverb is, "*Watch your words, for they become your thoughts. Watch your thoughts, for they create your world.*"

Emotional sobriety allows us to respond to the negative, stressful, and chaotic situations we all too often face in our daily lives. One of the most important elements of being sober-minded is being calm enough to ask for help. Sometimes, just the act of getting help brings focus and hope. I remember times when the simple presence of another person brought calm to the chaos, even though they had no idea how to help. The benefit of these people is that they often ask questions that lead to solutions.

How can other people see solutions that we cannot? Sometimes, it's as simple as emotional investment. While you have a high emotional investment, which causes stress and emotional thinking, they have little to no emotional investment so that they can think logically and rationally. A high emotional investment is when you are so deeply concerned about the outcome that you are no longer logically invested, and the very outcome of your feelings depends on the outcome of the circumstances. This means that you are at high risk of losing control of your emotions.

Chaos causes emotional thinking, which temporarily closes down our logic center. Therefore, enlisting the help of people who think logically is key to resisting chaos, shame, secrecy, and stress.

Being problem-focused increases stress and chaos, while problem-solving decreases them since it gives us back control. However, problem-solving does not necessarily eliminate stress and chaos altogether. We are looking to regain more control until we have enough control to handle the stress and chaos, and then it is either over or we have mastery over it.

We now know that sobriety is really the exercise of becoming calm. We then recruit our logical minds to take over problem-solving instead of emotional problem-focusing. So, pray and focus on hope.

A Note on Venting

Venting is the release of pressure. Some machines have a pressure release valve to vent their contents before a catastrophic failure occurs, which can, in a few cases, result in an explosion.

We have all seen someone explode emotionally. I have done it more than a few times. The tension caused by chaos is designed to build up until we do something we did not intend to do. The purpose of venting is to limit the built-up pressure that can come out in unexpectedly harmful ways.

It is okay to vent. In fact, the only way to deal with chaos is to talk about it openly. Scripture even says *And have no fellowship with the unfruitful works of darkness, but rather expose them.* – Eph 5:11 NKJV. When we are suffering because of something being done to us, being open about it is how we begin the healing process. There are a fair number of prayers in Scripture that are simply a person venting. Many of King David's prayers are venting prayers. He talks openly about his enemies and the troubles they have caused him. This is one reason he kept his sanity when other people would have given up.

The goal of venting is to clear the air of the emotions and how they are affecting us. It is not being problem-focused. It is identifying the problem in order to allow the mind to move from the painful emotional state into the logical state where problem-solving can take place.

Problem → Pain → Venting → Clearing the Mind → Problem-Solving

This is how we should use venting in our strategy to deal with chaos. When chaos delivers us a problem that leads to pain, then we can release those toxic emotions through venting, which will clear the mind of the swirl of emotions. Once the mind is clear, then we can move into our logical mind to begin addressing how to solve the problem.

Prayer:

"Dear heavenly Father, please infuse my mind with the spirit of hope and love. Show me how to love myself and see things that give me hope. I love You, In Yahushua/Jesus' name, amein."

Spiritual and Mental Realities

There is a whole matrix that affects a person's state of mind.

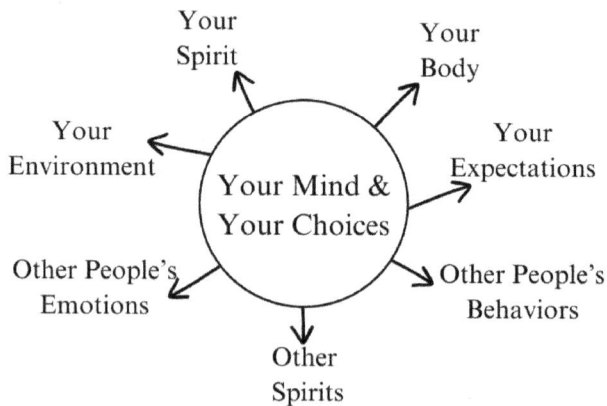

Your
Spirit

Your
Body

Your
Environment

Your Mind &
Your Choices

Your
Expectations

Other People's
Emotions

Other People's
Behaviors

Other
Spirits

The most important thing that affects your mind is your choices. Everything outside of your mind puts pressure on you to make certain choices, but you have the power to choose how you're going to engage, which means that you ultimately have the power to choose, not someone else. This does not mean that you are going to be unaffected. It just decides how you are going to move forward.

We often find ourselves in no-win situations. The power of choice means that we can own whatever we decide, even if we hate the decision. Owning gives us mental power over the situation and its future outcome. So if we make a no-win decision today, then tomorrow, we can work on turning it into a win-win. It doesn't matter if you know how to change it into a win-win. It's the attitude that defeats the no-win situation. Eventually, you will figure it out, often with the help of our loving heavenly Father.

Today's no-win can be tomorrow's win-win. It doesn't mean it's easy. It just means it's worth it. When things outside of your mind turn negative, you are automatically faced with a choice. "Do I go along with it? Ignore it? Or fight against it?" Once you pick, you have to decide how to implement your choice, and there are many ways to make that happen.

Making good decisions is extremely helpful. Sometimes, people will disagree with our good choices, occasionally when we least expect them. Almost any choice can create opposition. So, we might as well go with what's best for us. Those who care about us will be glad to hear it.

Remember that there are spirits of darkness whose only job is to create an environment where they influence people to steal, kill, and destroy. These people allow those negative thoughts to increase until they act. While you may not be susceptible to hurting others, you are susceptible to hurting yourself to prevent yourself from hurting someone else. Sadly, some people do harm people and then want to commit suicide out of guilt. We often act out of pain and then inflict pain. Some people get used to it and justify why they must do it. However, others have difficulty dealing with themselves when they hurt someone. When we hurt someone, we can face it, apologize, and make it right as much as possible. Or we can ignore it, hope it goes away, and live with the guilt.

People who are justified in their actions are not at all likely to feel guilt or remorse. The person hurt by them is likely never to receive an apology. Or worse, they can be re-victimized by the other person's justification and denial. When a person is self-justified, they can become one of the most damaging individuals to be around because they believe they are the victim, responding to other people hurting them. So, they fight back and hard. Even though there's nothing to fight. The real victim is usually victimized in ways they don't understand since they don't do that to others. Then, the confusion makes the victim even more emotionally vulnerable, especially to guilt.

Guilt is one of the most challenging emotions to deal with. It does not matter if your actions are right or wrong because someone can make you feel guilty for doing anything. "Some of the other negative emotions that can affect us to the point of suicide are sadness, hopelessness, anxiety, worthlessness, anger, irritability, and a lack of positive emotions." *Arslanoglou, Elizabeth, Samprit Banerjee, Joanna Pantelides, Laurie Evans, and Dimitris N Kiosses. "Negative Emotions and the Course of Depression during Psychotherapy in Suicidal Older Adults with Depression and Cognitive Impairment." The American journal of geriatric psychiatry : official journal of the American Association for Geriatric Psychiatry, December 2019. https:// www.ncbi.nlm.nih.gov/pmc/articles/PMC6985925/.*

All emotions are affected by our choices, including emotional choices. An emotional choice overrides our logic with strong feelings and makes us believe it will be purely satisfying, regardless of whether it is damaging. Yet, we can be affected by an emotion without giving in to it. Plus, we can change those emotions over time. Especially when we have a heavenly Father, we can pray to and talk with Him.

It takes focus on the things we want. Sabotage is a normal part of life. Man o' man, I wished I had been told that when I was younger. The only way to deal with it is to keep focus and understand that there is a cycle we all end up going through.

I call it the Spirit of the Confusion Cycle. The most interesting aspect of this cycle is that you may not feel any confusion. Its primary job is to confuse you about what is happening. It will whisper in your ear and the ears of others to damage your relationships, sabotage whatever it can, and cause other self-injurious behaviors.

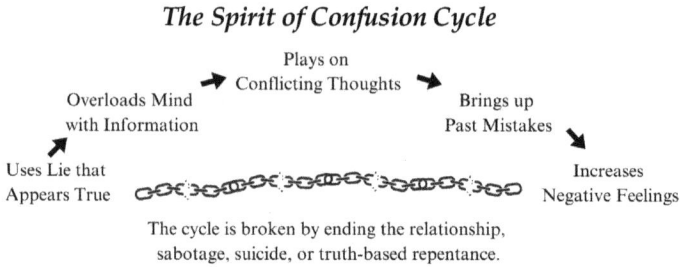

The Spirit of Confusion Cycle

Plays on
Conflicting Thoughts

Overloads Mind
with Information

Brings up
Past Mistakes

Uses Lie that
Appears True

Increases
Negative Feelings

The cycle is broken by ending the relationship,
sabotage, suicide, or truth-based repentance.

The first thing the devil ever said to us was designed to confuse the truth and lead us straight to death. He has to make his lie appear truth-like. Since it differs from the truth, information overloads and confuses the mind. Once in confusion, that evil spirit plays on the conflicting thoughts, which makes it much more difficult to make sound decisions. Past mistakes are brought up to increase negative feelings and guilt. Once in the cycle, more lies are brought in until the cycle breaks the person's mind. When the cycle breaks us, we either destroy ourselves or realize that we made a mistake and correct it.

The best way to begin truth-based repentance is to affirm to yourself that Yahweh loves you, forgives you, and helps you have a purpose. Yahweh also gives us people to help us leave the path of destruction and get us on the path of life. That purpose for your life reduces your susceptibility to sabotage and suicide. Since it does not eliminate it, you must protect your purpose because your enemies will start the confusion cycle on purpose. If your purpose is essential enough to you, you will find what you need in Yahweh, His Word, and yourself. Yahweh will bring other people and circumstances into your life to assist you with your purpose.

Susceptibility to Suicide

Being susceptible to suicide or other sabotage involves several different factors that are constantly changing. One day, you can be under a great deal of stress and have no thoughts of suicide. On another day, you'll be under a moderate amount of stress that triggers hopelessness, which puts you firmly on the path of chaos, leading you into the self-harm cycle.

"A trigger is the connection between the conscious mind and a buried painful memory." – Anonymous.

Triggers are different for everybody. Two people experiencing the same

16

trigger will cause one to consider serious self-harm while the other goes home to tear into a ½ gallon of ice cream. Although overeating ice cream is a form of self-harm, it's near the bottom for healthy people.

Sometimes, we know where a painful trigger comes from. Other times, it's buried in our subconscious mind. Often, triggers have physical symptoms, from a sense of foreboding to an outright panic attack.

What increases our susceptibility to suicide or sabotage is recognizing our triggers and our inappropriate responses to them while proudly refusing to deal with them. So, it saddens me that I have done the same thing more than once. As Prov 16:18a says, *"Pride goes before destruction..."* Dealing with pride issues, while very challenging, is the first step in dealing with triggers. We may feel justified when our logical minds disagree, especially seeing someone else do the same things.

The other trigger is an ongoing situation that you cannot resolve, where you are emotionally involved. This trigger worsens as time passes because you see the problem returning and know you do not have a satisfactory solution. This will constantly increase your stress.

Three of the most common triggers are abuse, disappointment, and tragedy.
1. Abuse: Treat (a person or animal) with cruelty or violence, esp. regularly or repeatedly. Use or treat in such a way as to cause damage or harm.
2. Disappointment: sadness or displeasure caused by the non-fulfillment of one's hopes or expectations.
3. Tragedy: an event causing great suffering, destruction, and distress, such as a severe accident, crime, or natural catastrophe.

Now that we've looked at the dictionary's definition of abuse, let's get down to brass tacks of relationship abuse. "All abuse comes down to the belief that one person needs to control another person or a group of people. The abuser is always self-justified in their need to gain and maintain their control, regardless of what type of control is used."*"Abusive Power and Control." Wikipedia, June 16, 2024. https://en.wikipedia.org/wiki/ Abusive_power_and_control.* That person feels the need to gain power and perceives the need to use that power over another person.

In my personal experience, the abuser will have some life-altering moments or moments where they felt powerless and out-of-control, so they now are emotionally invested in creating a life where they control as many factors as possible to regain that original sense of emotional safety by exerting their dominance over someone else. We need to understand that there is a world of difference between controlling a situation and being in control of a person. Controlling a situation means controlling another person's or people's potentially harmful behavior until the behavior is over. Then, the control is over. The control is focused on the behavior, not the person.

Abusers see the need to control the person or people to control their behavior. The "need" to continue to control the person or people remains long after the behavior has ceased. Abusers will continue to exert control, even when there is compliance, because they cannot allow the loss of control. They see this as a way to prevent harmful behavior.

When an abuser brings up your past mistakes, it's to remind you why they "must" maintain their control over you – to prevent you from failing again. Someone who is not abusive may bring up a past mistake to show you how much you have learned and grown or to encourage you not to quit learning and growing.

Because an abuser will justify their abuse, they honestly believe they are controlling the problem, not the person. Therefore, getting an abuser to see their behavior as "abuse" is extremely difficult, at best. They only see "cause and effect" from their point of view. "If you hadn't done this, then I wouldn't have had to do that," goes the rationalization. I remember several of these conversations. I believe this blame game is a serious factor in suicide because the victim is left without resolution or clarity. The problem is never resolved, and the victim cannot see the cycle of abuse. Since the abuser does not see themselves as the problem, whatever negative behavior the victim has is solely the victim's fault, not theirs. Abusers have remarkably clear consciences.

The only time a victim can get an abuser to admit wrongdoing is if the abuse can be made evident to them. If the abuser has given the victim a black eye, then the problem is obvious, and the abuser may even be afraid that "other people" will blame the abuser, which causes them to want to appease the victim. This is the "honeymoon phase" in the reconciliation cycle of abuse.

The Cycle of Abuse

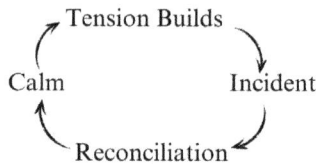

```
              Tension Builds
        Calm              Incident
              Reconciliation
```

Tension Builds: Stress grows from the pressures of daily life or other points of conflict. The victim may attempt to reduce tension by complying with the abuser.

Incident: Verbal, emotional, physical, or sexual abuse occurs. This includes anger, intimidation, threats, and other forms of abuse.

Reconciliation: The abuser apologizes, shows remorse, and often begs for forgiveness. They may shower the victim with love and affection, then promise that the abuse will never happen again.

Calm: The relationship enters a period of calm where the abuser stops or slows. The abuser may continue to ask for forgiveness, or make positive gestures. These tend to reduce in sincerity over time.

As in the case of financial abuse, the victim may know there's enough money for them to buy an item, but the abuser will deliberately spend the money on "necessities," so not only will the victim not get what they asked for, but will be made to feel selfish for even asking. The abuser will feel like a victim if the actual victim calls them out for their manipulation. Then, the victim will almost always be re-victimized when the abuser explains since the abuser will point out how selfish and self-serving the victim is.

Abusers always put their victims in win-lose situations because they have either been put in or simply perceived that they were placed in the same win-lose situation. It's not to say that they will never create a win-win. The win-win will only come when they are comfortable controlling their victim. The win-lose creates an imbalance to keep the victim off guard and powerless so that they may effectively defend themselves against the victim's predictable resistance. Both the victim and the abuser believe they are equally the victim.

One of the biggest questions people have, which increases the victim's sense of isolation, is, "Why didn't you say anything?" First of all, victims often do. Second is that the abusers are very good at creating doubt to the point that the victim believes that they are to blame, at least in some way, and doubt does the rest. Even when the victim sees a problem, the doubt prevents the victim from fully self-advocating, which creates doubt in the people around them that a problem exists. Abusers rely on the fact that most folks just don't want to get involved in someone else's messy relationship. Suicide becomes an option because the victim feels so powerless that they think the only thing they have the power to change is whether they live or die.

Disappointments and tragedies create the same feelings of powerlessness. Even though there is no abuse, the inability to control things outside of our power to do so gives us that feeling of being victimized. It is the hopelessness from the realization that we are more impotent to prevent or change things than we believe. Since we often think we have more control than we do.

Because of this, many people like to use the Serenity Prayer by Reinhold Niebuhr,"Yah grant me the serenity to accept the things I cannot change, courage to change the things I can, and the wisdom to know the difference."

We need to find peace when we feel things are out of control. Praying puts us in contact with someone interested in helping us and can do so. Yahweh is not a wish-master. Instead, He is a loving Ruler and Father who wants things to go well for the one He cares about. He sent His Son to do what we could not: rescue us from death by beating death at its own game. It's His peace that we have to rely on.

Over-Idealization and Rejection

How often do we want someone or something so strongly that we are crushed when we are rejected by what we were idolizing? We can easily put someone or something on a pedestal only to discover that they do not feel the same way about us. While rejection can be very stressful, it is often potentiated by feelings caused by over-idealizing the person or situation. When we idolize someone, we lower ourselves while lifting them. There is an emotional imbalance. The idolized person cannot meet our needs, even if they want to do so. Most of the time, they do not. It is not healthy.

The younger we are, the more likely we are to engage in idolizing. Although, plenty of adults do the same thing. However, the younger we are, the more traumatic the rejection can be, which means that suicidal ideation becomes worse.

Rejection can strike at the core of our being like nothing else can because it can make us feel so woefully inadequate. That emotional power imbalance can cause an identity crisis. We believed we were on the same level, only to discover that we were not. When we are so emotionally invested in the outcome, we become blind to the other possibilities, such as this is not a good fit. Hope is a beautiful thing. However, we can slip past the point of being hopeful into over-idealizing the situation. It is very easy to put our emotions into someone else's place and then discover that they are not okay with that.

I remember having a fantasy about asking a girl out. When she rejected me, I understood that I had not attempted to build any kind of relationship with her on any level. So, I was nothing more than a familiar face. Things might have been different if I had treated her like a person instead of a player in my imagination.

We often do not think about the consequences of rejection and what we will do after that. The times in which I thought through a situation and planned for rejection were times when I felt prepared for the "no" because I had a game plan. When I pinned my hopes solely on being accepted, then the rejection could be traumatizing.

Abuse is a Form of Rejection

You are probably asking yourself, "How is abuse a form of rejection?" That's a great question. Abusers reject our value as an equal human being. They see other people as pawns, not people. They create an emotional power imbalance. There is something about us that they want, while at the same time, they are rejecting a core piece of who we are. Being rejected as an equal and accepted as an inferior is more damaging than outright rejection.

Abusers go to great lengths to hide this fact from their victims. They create the facade of equality by telling us what we want to hear. However, their actions reject that notion as they tear us down to ensure we don't become a threat. They are threatened by someone who is their equal. They only "trust" us when they have us in an inferior position. That way, they can control the outcome of our behavior. They reject us for who we are and then try to conform us to their image or ideal. This is why abuse is so difficult to comprehend because it is an ad hoc mixture of acceptance and rejection. There are multiple levels to the mind games, depending on the complexity of the abuser.

Principle of Quitting

We are often bombarded with lists of things to do to be successful. Seven things to do to be happy, lose weight, make more money, etc. Occasionally, we have to stop doing things to be successful at something. There are things we do that sabotage ourselves, regardless of what others do to us. These are things that we must quit to be successful.

It is difficult to quit an abusive relationship. Sometimes, it even feels impossible. The key is to make it as simple as possible. Certain types of quitting will help anyone. Even if you are not experiencing abuse but are still feeling depressed and having suicidal thoughts, the following things will help. I wished that I had had them sooner.

Rob Dial mentions 5 Things to Quit:

1. Trying to please everyone
2. Fearing change
3. Living in the past
4. Putting yourself down
5. Over-thinking

While these five things might not specifically speak to your situation, these cover a majority of issues that plague our minds. If you look more carefully at the circumstances you are going through, you may very well find that one of those things to quit does indeed cover your situation.

Are you trying to please someone who is putting you down? Do you fear the consequences of making a meaningful change that could improve your life? Do you find comfort in the past instead of living today? Are other people's opinions more important than your opinion of yourself? When there is a problem, do you go over and over it in your mind, sometimes until you are mentally exhausted?

Maybe your problem is not covered in those five things to quit. You know what your issue is. How are you handling it? Is how you are handling it going to take care of it successfully? If what you are doing is not working, then you have to quit the unsuccessful behavior.

The problem with quitting anything is that you have to replace it with something. Otherwise, there will be an emotional vacuum that will be refilled with your old behavior. You'll just simply go back to doing what you were doing before. However, when you replace it with something else, you stop thinking about whatever you are quitting. It's important because whatever you think about will help or sabotage you. It's where you will put your energy and time.

When faced with a situation that troubles you and creates anxiety and fear, look for positive solutions. Putting your mind on finding solutions lessens anxiety and fear. Why? Because it gives you control over the problem instead of the problem having power over you. Whether you like taking a math class or not, you soon learn that every math problem has a solution. It's a matter of working it out. Problems are the same way. You may not like the problem, but it has a solution. Some solutions require more help than you have within yourself. Prayer connects you with the One who has solutions.

Here are 5 Things to Start:
1. Set healthy boundaries
2. Plan for change
3. Live for today, plan for tomorrow
4. Complement yourself and others
5. Pray and learn about your life from Scripture.

We often start wanting to please people because we know that helping them is what we want them to do for us, but we find out that we are being taken advantage of instead. By setting healthy boundaries, we can still be helpful without being taken advantage of or manipulated. This not only increases our self-respect but also requires them to respect us. While we may not know what to plan for, we can mentally prepare to expect changes. This gives our mind flexibility so that, when a change comes, we are not shocked and left unprepared.

We are always going to think about the past. Everyone does. The difference between emotionally healthy people and the unhealthy is where, in time, their mind lives. Emotionally healthy people are focused on taking care of today and planning to make tomorrow as beneficial as possible. We don't have to worry about yesterday or tomorrow. We just take care of what is here now. This takes much of the pressure off of things we cannot control.

Emotionally speaking, we are either thinking negatively or positively but not simultaneously. When you choose to be positive, giving compliments is the best way to walk that out. First, focus on yourself. This will provide you with the emotional energy to give compliments to others. It's an excellent way to live out the Bible's command to "love others as you love yourself." Loving and complementing yourself raises your emotional strength to deal with the negativity others will throw at you.

Complementing others gives you even more confidence in dealing with other people. When you compliment someone, you raise their esteem in your eyes while making it possible for them to do the same for you. It is difficult for someone to tear you down while you are building them up. Plus, complimenting someone makes it easier to provide them with more help if needed. When you help someone who is acting like an enemy, then it gives them emotional permission to see you as a friend. Which is why the Messiah said to "love your enemies." Seeing someone as an enemy is tough when they are helping you.

Using the Negative

Everybody acknowledges that telling a child not to touch scalding water is very important because it will burn them. That's a classic example of using something negative for a positive purpose. One really good thing to do is to remind yourself of the good things that you will lose when you engage in sabotaging behavior or contemplate suicide. When you think about what you want, ask yourself, "Will this *[negative behavior]* take away what I want?" By thinking about the negative consequences of where your thoughts will lead you, you can take control and push your thoughts where you want to go. Yes, it takes practice, but practice makes you better.

Focus Predicts your Future

Since your mind can only focus on one thing at a time, you can be problem-focused or problem-solving. Because you cannot do both simultaneously, you select the trajectory of your life; even if you are in the midst of the most awful circumstances, you can survive. One of the benefits is that you will have a cool story to tell. Another benefit is the ability to help people you currently cannot help. Many people don't trust the advice from folks who have not experienced similar problems. Why? Because their advice is not tested in the fire of adversity.

When I hear stories about people who lived through the Nazi Holocaust of World War Two, I know that when they talk about things like being able to forgive a prison guard who tortured them, then it means that I can forgive someone who has wronged me or go through any other misery.

Most survivors of terrible experiences survived because they transitioned from problem-focused to problem-solving. One of my favorite books as a child was about another child, a refugee in China during the Japanese occupation. Now I realize why it was the first book I read twice. The boy was constantly problem-solving amid a life-or-death struggle. He was afraid but chose to overcome instead of giving in to fear.

Spiritual and Mental Bonds

When we are in relationships with people, whether family, friends, or co-workers, we create mental and spiritual bonds. We may be able to recognize an emotional bond, but often, we don't recognize a spiritual one. A spiritual bond increases the emotional and mental bonds. We just need to figure out exactly how. One thing that seems obvious to me is that people who are accepting and supportive tend to have spirits around them that are like that, which enhances their behavior. Conversely, someone who criticizes and complains will have spirits that empower that behavior.

Interestingly, this is why we can change from person to person—becoming different around different people. Their spirits may affect us in ways we do not realize or guard against. This is why we can have so many different emotional experiences with people and why things can change for no apparent reason.

Think about the times when your opinion has changed when nothing else did. A spirit likely communicated with your spirit, which communicated with your mind. This is why we must "...*bringing every thought into captivity...*" 2 Cor 10:5 NKJV Some thoughts are sabotage, while other thoughts help us grow. We must examine every thought and reject those that will damage ourselves and others. Yes, this is work. It is not as complicated as some folk make it, though. It's still true that you get out of life what you put into it.

This Book of the Law shall not depart from your mouth, but you shall meditate in it day and night, that you may observe to do according to all that is written in it. For then you will make your way prosperous, and then you will have good success. - Joshua 1:8 NKJV When the law of life is applied, it naturally resists the law of death and the practitioners of death. Your mind, as you pray, will be connected to the Yahweh. Who you choose to have in your life will exponentiate either the good or the bad. *Do not be deceived, "Evil company corrupts good habits."* - 1 Cor 15:33 NKJV With that bad company comes the spirits that support them. Thankfully, the opposite is also true.

Chaos hits everybody when we least expect it, but we can be prepared by filling our minds and souls with life before those events occur. Refilling our minds with life after surviving a chaotic episode is equally important.

Things to do Daily

1. Pray to Yahweh, the Life-Giver.
2. Read His Word.
3. Associate with people who are life-oriented.
4. Avoid people and situations that drain your life.
5. Focus on your life-affirming goals.

Prayer:

"Dear heavenly Father, please grant me the spirit of life to help me focus on the life You gave me. Lead me today to do the things that You have set before me. Guide my mind and hands to create a life worth living. In Yahushua/Jesus's Name, amein."

My Story

So, at this point, I should be honest about why I am writing this book. The truth is that I have had four episodes where I was very close to committing suicide. I do not want a 5th episode. This book is partly my therapy. It also gives me hope that what I have experienced can help others.

I was 11 years old when I first wanted to commit suicide. I don't remember exactly why, but it was a lonely time. My Grandfather Crowe had recently died at the age of 72. I was not ready for him to be gone. He was a mentor and someone I looked up to very much. It tore my heart out losing him. Losing my grandfather changed my perception of where I wanted to be. Nine to ten months earlier, during summer break, my grandfather led me to Christ in his Southern Baptist church in Oklahoma. I had spent nearly three months with my grandparents and did not want to return to New Mexico.

A few months later, I heard the volunteer fire department radio tone for a call up the street. My dad was home, and when I heard what kind of call it was, I knew there was a chance that he would not let me go. It was a possible suicide. I ran out the door with his jump kit (a first aid kit with extra supplies for EMTs) and ran up to the trailer at the address given by dispatch. That's when I got cold feet and stopped to wait for my dad. To my surprise, he did not tell me to stay outside, so I followed him. An older teenage male was hanging from the closet rod in the back bedroom. All the clothes had been removed.

My dad cut him down and began to assess him. It was too late. I had the jump kit open and was disappointed that there was nothing that I could hand him to save the teen's life. His family arrived a few minutes later. Instinctively, I turned to usher them out of the room, and at the same moment, my dad asked me to do the same thing. Thankfully, they turned to leave. I was glad to go with them. I went back and forth to check on my dad. When he did not need my help, I would leave. The rest of the time, I waited outside for the ambulance to come to take the body away. I carried my dad's jump kit back to the house, a very different person.

The Loneliness

I wish I could remember more about what happened that year. I was lonely. I had friends at school but not at home. I helped my mom around the house and with shopping, but I rarely played with anyone. When I walked the dog, I was alone in the mile-high desert of Albuquerque. Honestly, I had too much time to think. The suicide a few months earlier had more of an effect on me than I realized.

As the school year dragged on, I was less enchanted about life despite living in the Land of Enchantment. As I struggled with depression, I think those two deaths made me think of death as an escape. I sincerely believed that my Grandfather Crowe was in heaven, and heaven sounded like a much better place to be than here. I frequently looked into the sky and wanted to be lifted up there. So, I devised a plan of escape.

My parents had just started allowing me to stay home alone. The first night, I cuddled on the couch with my dog, who was not much of a cuddler, and tried to watch TV while being scared out of my wits at every little sound. As time went on, I grew more confident about being alone. Then, when I decided that I no longer wanted to be here, I looked forward to one particular night when I convinced my parents to let me stay home.

I planned how I wanted things to go for a couple of weeks. When the night came, my parents agreed to let me stay home alone. They took my younger sister and went to some regularly scheduled meetings, I think at the fire department. I was calm and focused. I did not rush. After ensuring they did not return because someone needed to remember something, I walked over to the kitchen counter and pulled out a sharp, pointed steak knife. Earlier in the week, I chose that knife over any of the others that might have worked. My dad kept it very sharp, and it fit in my small hands nicely. Plus, it had a skinny blade, so it wouldn't need to make a large hole.

Emotionally, I felt like my life was finally in my control. In retrospect, this is why I was so calm. For the first time, I took control of the events surrounding it. I was deciding where I truly wanted to be – not here. So, as I held the knife in my hands, I felt an empowerment that I had never felt before. So, it felt good to turn it towards my chest. This was a moment of liberation. I put the tip of the blade near my sternum between two ribs that I thought would be about where my heart should be. I hadn't thought about this part, though. So, I pondered on what I should do next. I was afraid I wouldn't be able to shove it through my shirt and chest. I looked at the kitchen counter and thought that I could lean in on it so that my momentum would drive the knife into my heart.

As I rocked back and forth, trying to think of how to do it so as not to be more painful than it was going to be, I began to picture in my head what my parents would find when they came home. I could see myself lying dead in a pool of blood on the kitchen floor. That part did not bother me in the least. The part that did bother me was the emotions that would wash over them seeing their son dead. I remember turning my head slightly to the left toward the front door of our trailer, and then, imagining them walking through that door to find me dead. That must have been when I connected the moment the teen's parents walked into their trailer. I knew I couldn't do that to my parents. Defeated, I put the knife back in the drawer.

Lesson Learned?

No, not really. I didn't want to endure the pain of thrusting the knife into my heart. It's likely that I would have missed and simply would have had to call 911 while having trouble breathing and speaking. Then, I would have had to explain why I did what I did. My choice to live was more for someone else's benefit than my own. I did not come away from the experience with a newfound vigor to live. I just didn't want to die—well, at least not in the way that I chose. I couldn't see any other options, so why not just live?

Later, in middle school, I had another bought of depression and suicidal ideation. Honestly, I don't remember much about it.

In the first semester of my junior year, I lost my way. I had spent another enjoyable summer with my grandmother, and as usual, I was not happy about returning home. Each year, coming home got harder and harder. While I don't remember the details, I became angry at Yahweh for some selfish reason and turned my back on Him. All I remember is that it happened while I was in the youth group at church. As an introvert, naturally, I didn't tell anyone. This would be one of the main reasons why I struggled emotionally for most of my youth and early adulthood.

For three months, I would go to church with an agnostic chip on my shoulder. I knew Yahweh existed; I just did not want to have anything to do with Him. It felt freeing at first. I was on my own and in control of my life once again. Whatever that means. (It probably means I was an impetuous, spoiled brat needing correction.) Then, the darkness began to overtake me. The depression and the despair grew until I thought, once again, that suicide was the answer. It was not. Thankfully, I figured that out before doing something easier than using a knife.

I wish I could tell you that I had an immediate turnaround. It took several more months for me to repair my relationship with my heavenly Father. However, He gave me friends to hang out with and an amazing skit to take to the state German conference. I came in third place, but a lot of my peers thought I should have won first place. That was an absolute honor. Plus, I met a cool girl that night, too.

As I said, I struggled into adulthood. Depression took its toll. I often entertained suicidal thoughts. As I matured, I wasn't as committed to actually ending my life. It probably helped that I was married and had two children. However, I wasn't happy and didn't know what to do with myself. I knew what I wanted, but that seemed on another plane of existence.

My wife, children, and I moved to El Paso, TX—a place I never wanted to be. However, I met a friend at the local Messianic synagogue. He was my first real friend at that point in my life. I would go over to his house and just hang out. It was such a blessing since I had not had that in years. Sadly, his mom died. It was a hard time for him. I would let him talk and vent as needed. For some reason, his sisters were giving him a hard time about their mother's will.

He explained some of the issues. Everything seemed very straightforward, except the part about his sisters' response to the will. They did not like their mother's decisions about who got what. I knew he was frustrated by it all.

On one Sabbath morning at the synagogue, I heard the shocking news that he had committed suicide. I was stunned. I couldn't believe it. As I was trying to run through my mind everything that he told me, I just couldn't seem to remember anything that sounded like something he should kill himself over. That was just my opinion. At the funeral, I was still in shock. This was a truly good man whose body lay in that casket. He was a real friend, and I was a friend to him. When it was over, I broke down, sobbing uncontrollably. A couple of folks from our congregation consoled me. It was the only funeral where I just lost it. Probably because his death was so unexpected, at least to me, anyway, and I was going to miss his friendship.

That's when I began to understand that I could never commit suicide or even let it be a thought in my mind. For the first time, I understood what it meant to survive the loss of someone close to you who had committed suicide. I was never going to put anyone else through that.

I Became Suicide Sober

From that time on, I did not struggle with suicidal ideation. Even when things would get tough, I knew that suicide was a cop-out and would not tolerate it. However, one interesting thing would happen to me from time to time. I would get this desire to kill myself just out of the blue. I wouldn't think about it, and this feeling would wash over me. I realized that these thoughts were not my own. Spiritual beings implanted them. These demons would somehow place these thoughts in my head.

Once I realized these thoughts did not originate with me, I could take them captive and rebuke the demons behind them. As quickly as they came, they left. That was such a liberating moment. It made me feel like I was in control of my life and in a positive, life-affirming way.

I wished I had been better in other areas of my life. Sadly, some of my personal life was self-destructive. My first marriage was not affirming, and I did not decently handle her attitude. We needed marriage counseling, but she shifted the blame towards me, and that was her choice. Instead of being mature and trying to discuss our issues, we started to ignore each other. Things got worse, and I got worse. Thankfully, suicide was not an issue.

Because I was self-destructing emotionally in my marriage, she rightfully decided to divorce me. I was grateful that it was over. While we both sabotaged the marriage, I did more so. Although I figured that she completely blamed me for the divorce, years later, I discovered that she understood that she was partly to blame. I respect her for that.

The Next Phase

While I didn't own all my mistakes, I began to own what I could admit. That was a start. Slowly but surely, I began rebuilding my life and attempted to rebuild my relationship with my children. We got along well while they were still in school. I had them once a week and could take them to Oklahoma for several weeks each year to see their grandparents.

As I got more involved in a Messianic congregation in Denver, I became close to an assistant pastor couple. The husband became my mentor. He helped me see some of the areas of my life that still needed cleaning up. I was still a mess but was making real progress. This was a golden era of my life. I was lonely and wanted to be married, but I was having fun and even maturing.

The one crack in my life was that I still did not like myself. I cannot remember a time when I enjoyed myself. However, this was missing from the list of things being dealt with. I wish it was addressed then, but it wasn't.

I dated a little during this time, but I only managed to have one girlfriend during these years. I had a couple of close calls that didn't pan out, and the loneliness was a pain. However, each year, my life got better and more satisfying.

Then It Happened

I saw this lovely woman walk into our congregation one day. I became friends with her and found out that she was married. I was disappointed. However, that disappointment faded away as we became friends. She talked about her marriage, which was headed for a divorce to me. It was also clear that the divorce was not going to be immediate.

She would come and go. Sometimes, I would not see her for a while. I didn't take much notice because I was paying more attention to the single ladies who were in attendance. The times that she did make it to service, I usually greeted her. I felt a comradery with her that I did not feel with the other gals. Eventually, I began teaching Shabbat classes, and she signed up for everyone I taught. At that point, she became a regular attendee of our congregation. Occasionally, we would talk about the class topic or just different things in general.

Some time passed, and she told me that her husband had moved out of her house and into his mistress's house. He finally decided to divorce her. It wasn't his first affair. He cheated on her with at least two other women over several years. Yet, she seemed fit to forgive him and stand for the restoration of her marriage.

It didn't take long for us to become involved. During the months that she was waiting for the divorce to be finalized, we became a couple, and we seemed to instantly bond. It was a whirlwind romance—quite intense—and I really enjoyed the intensity. We had several arguments related to scriptural interpretation, but there were no arguments about life or how we would pursue it. Those things were worked out without fussing or fighting. It seemed to be an easy relationship.

After her divorce was finalized, I asked her to marry me. We took some time to get marriage counseling with my mentor and his wife. That was a blessed time. For the most part, I really enjoyed it. She complained about it at times, but we were faithful to the process.

When the wedding came, I was in heaven, and the honeymoon, thanks to a generous aunt, was like heaven on earth. I could not have asked for a better honeymoon. It lasted a week in the mountains of western Colorado. We had so many memorable experiences. I felt connected to her.

As Time Goes By

Three months after the wedding, she sat me down to tell me that we were pregnant. This was a surprise since she told me beforehand that she didn't think it was possible that she could get pregnant because she and her first husband wanted a second child and tried everything without success. The doctors even gave up. What a miracle! Our son was born two days before our first wedding anniversary. What a blessing that time was.

We left the congregation where we met. She was no longer happy there and wanted to have a home group. We started one. A mutual friend of ours from that congregation eventually joined us. Things were going well. After a few months, our friend moved to a small city 45 minutes to the south, where she was taking care of her aunt. Occasionally, we would take the home group members to her aunt's spacious home. It was really nice. We met in the finished basement, where we could be rambunctious without offending her aunt's sensibilities. She needed help understanding her niece's Jewish ideas about the Christian Christ. Not much later, our friend invited us to her aunt's house to talk to her about something important. We went without knowing what the conversation was about, but we had no worries—we probably should have.

Our friend was older than us and very astute. She had noticed my wife's behavior towards me and was unhappy. During the opening of the conversation, she told my wife that she had a Jezebel spirit because she often usurped my authority and wanted to be in control while remaining in the background so that she would not have to take responsibility for her decisions. I was relieved because I knew something was wrong but could not put my finger on it since she had tried to mask her behavior. My wife hotly denied it, and her daughter defended her as we talked. I was in shock. The problem, which was below the surface but was slowly beginning to become worse, was exposed. This should have been the night that rescued our marriage before things became bad. That's not what happened.

Anytime anything went wrong, I would admit it and deal with it. Then, we would work to try to expel any lingering demons. I appreciated doing this with my wife. It made me feel spiritually clean and kept the marriage on track. However, she did not do this in return. When our friend brought up a real problem, my wife did the exact opposite of what she expected me to do in the same situation. There was none of the humility my wife expected from me when

I was in the same boat. Instead, she was embittered towards our friend and kept denying the allegation. I did not want to fail my second marriage like I did my first. I did not know that she saw herself in a completely different manner. Since her daughter was defending her, it only reinforced her false paradigm.

Sadly, even though it had been over a year, I was still in the honeymoon phase. This may be why I tolerated her berating me for 40 minutes of the 45-minute drive home. Things cooled off. This marriage was still substantially better than my first one, so we seemed to make things work.

One of the weird things I noticed was how she defended her abusive father. He did not abuse her. He seemed to get off on yelling at her mother. We lived upstairs. The house's second floor was turned into a lovely apartment that we rented. I could still hear his yelling. One day, I was fed up with it. So, as I marched towards the stairway door, my wife blocked me. Boy, was I surprised.

Not my wife. She defended the abuser and refused to help the victim. I think it was here that the marriage began unraveling, but I didn't realize it. This happened two more times. Later, she didn't think I was listening as she was crying to her daughter about how mean her dad was to her mom. I was furious at her hypocrisy. Yet, I never told her.

A year later, without her knowledge, I confronted her dad about it. He was shocked. Then he shocked me by saying that she was his wife and that he had the right to treat her however he saw fit. I discovered that he saw no problem with what he was doing. Then, I remembered what my wife had said about her dad when I had wanted to confront him earlier. "Oh, he's just old school. That's the way he was raised."

I think it was during this time that my self-respect slowly began to diminish as I failed to stop an abuser. My wife continued to work on "my issues." No matter how hard we tried, I could never seem to get rid of my issues. We even paid good money to spiritual counselors to pray the demons out of me. I would get better. Then she would say that I was worse again, and the cycle would repeat. Even when the spiritual counselors said I was done, she would somehow "magically" find something else. Then, all of us would get back to trying to figure it out. When she was satisfied, then and only then was it over.

A Fresh Start

My wife's sister spent several months trying to talk us into moving to Montana. Since I had some vacation time built up, we decided to go and check it out. Even though we thought it would be nice, we practically decided against moving there before leaving Colorado. My sister-in-law's spread was nicer than we expected. It was like a lovely vacation ranch rather than a traditional ranch, and those few days were unexpectedly enjoyable.

After returning to Colorado, we talked and decided to move to Montana. I cashed out my retirement from work. After making plans with my sister-in-law and her husband, we moved with their help. I started to learn how to take care of some of their animals. I would gladly feed the chickens and gather eggs most mornings and evenings. Occasionally, the rooster would try to assert his dominance. It was more entertaining than anything, and the fresh eggs were so delightful.

My favorite thing turned out to be milking the goat. My sister-in-law spent a week showing me how to do it. While it was fairly straightforward, it could turn into a mess if I didn't follow the steps properly. I made a few mistakes, but learning the hard way was more disappointing than disastrous. My sister-in-law noticed that the goats seemed to be comfortable with me. She had trained other people to milk the goats before so hearing her say that I was the only one who got this far with the herd was nice.

My wife's daughter and her husband also moved in with us. She was pregnant, so the fresh goat's milk was a huge blessing.

Things were going better than expected. One day, my brother-in-law invited me to his fifth wheel, which he preferred over the ranch house. We talked, which I have always enjoyed because he was like a brother. During the conversation, he specifically brought up my wife's behavior towards me. He had noticed her Jezebel spirit and counseled me to do something about it. Although I agreed with him, I had no idea how to do that. Nothing had improved since that night at our friend's house years earlier. She must have known something was up because she grilled me about it later. This was the beginning of the end of her relationship with her sister since it was her sister's husband who had the audacity to bring it up.

After the baby's birth, things became noticeably more tense between the two. One day, we all had a big family meeting. It did not go well, as one could imagine. The real reason for the issues should have been said. Naturally, my wife was angry that I did not defend her that night. I would have if I could have. Of course, I couldn't tell her that.

Soon after that last meeting, we all moved to Butte. I missed the ranch, but we found a cool house for both families. I found a job that I liked very much, working with troubled youth. I was quickly promoted to the Recreational Therapy Department. I thrived in that environment. Sadly, my relationship with my wife was not thriving. We were hanging on, and some days were better than others.

At this point, I wouldn't say that it was bad. One night, we had an unexpected night of passion. I really felt like we were reconnecting. As I lay there feeling very open to her emotionally, she began to bring up some issues that were bothering her. Well, it turned into a 45-minute session of bashing me emotionally in the subtle but equally effective damaging way that she would never tolerate anyone doing to her. That night, when the gripe session was over, so was my ability to ever feel any real emotional connection with her. She permanently destroyed what was left of my willingness to be vulnerable and open towards her. Now, I would be forever guarded toward her, never trusting, always very cautious. No matter what she did after that, I would look at her behavior in at least a slightly suspicious way.

Another Fresh Start?

My son-in-law had been a professional firefighter in another state. However, nepotism was rampant in Montana. We did not know this prior to moving up there. He kept applying and even testing with different departments. An ambulance company north of us nearly hired him, or so they made him think. Naturally, he became frustrated that he could not find anything. It became worse when he talked to another out-of-stater. This is when he found out about nepotism. The guy told him he had tested out as the number one candidate in all categories but has yet to hear back. When he called them back two weeks later, they told him they had given the position to someone else without further explanation.

So, my son-in-law returned to New Mexico and tested with two different departments. He was the number one candidate for the second one. Unlike Montana, that department gave him whatever he wanted. Since we all moved to Montana, we moved to New Mexico together. Clovis was our destination. I had heard of it but had never been close to there. Thankfully, it was decent, with only a few thousand folks less than Butte. I came to miss the mountains of Butte. However, that was the very least of my problems.

New Problems

We all found a four-bedroom, two-story house in a good neighborhood. Our two younger children made friends quickly, and the grandchildren enjoyed us taking them to the different parks close by. For a time, things were relatively decent. My relationship with my wife was stable, and I found a job that paid the bills. Although the relationship was stable, there was no healing from what happened in Montana. We just moved forward, and that was good enough.

My son-in-law's dad lived south of Albuquerque. His ex-wife had just moved back to Albuquerque. They carpooled for a couple of visits since they both wanted to see their son, and we all enjoyed it when they came to visit. It was a blessing.

During the summer, his dad once brought his canoe. We all drove to a lake a couple of hours away and found a spot away from the crowds. It was perfect because there was a shallow inlet where the younger children could safely play in the clear water. At first, things seemed perfectly normal. I took a turn in the canoe with my youngest son. We didn't go out too far since a few motorboats were speeding on the other side, and my son was content to stay reasonably close to shore.

My wife was in the water with the little ones, and I went to the picnic tables to get some refreshments. That's when I noticed that she was looking at him for unusually long periods. Something that I had never seen her do before. I didn't know what to think, and maybe I was being weird or something. So I decided to take a walk in the rolling hills nearby. If I was simply imagining her odd behavior, then randomly popping out and seeing what she was doing should clear things up.

Well, four of the five times I randomly looked to see what she was up to turned out to be the same as before. Seeing that the young ones in the water beside her should be commanding her attention made me realize something was up. She wasn't simply glancing. It was staring. It was a new behavior. I wish I could say that I was jealous. I simply was not. That even bothered me, although it didn't bother me very much. After that bad night in Montana, I guess I saw it as a potential way out, even though I wasn't thinking about a way out during that trip. Honestly, it was a surreal moment—almost an out-of-body type moment.

Maybe five weeks later, she and I were alone in the house, doing something in the dining room. She started weirdly talking to me, and it seemed like she was deliberately trying to push my buttons to make me angry. Then, calmly, with a slight smile, she flatly said, "You want to hit me. Don't you?" I was getting angry indeed, although hitting someone when I was angry was something I had never done as an adult. I was too emotionally charged to realize, at the moment, how bizarre her behavior was. This was another new thing to pop up. Since I was not in my right mind, I just walked away. I had worked enough with violent clients that hitting someone while angry was not my way of doing things. I was shocked, a little hurt, but mostly bewildered.

When fall arrived, my son-in-law's dad started visiting regularly, as he would get time off from work for holidays. Every time he visited, my wife would make him a cot. She did the same for his ex-wife a couple of times when she came without him and also for my dad's visit. However, something was different about the time before his visit. It was her stress level. If it was only his ex-wife coming by herself or my dad, her stress levels were normal. If he were coming with his ex-wife, her stress levels would increase. If he came alone, her stress levels were much, much higher.

After a few months, when I heard her daughter yell out, "He's coming to visit this weekend, " I would get sick. I was no longer glad he was coming because I knew she would take out her stress on me until he arrived. On the Friday prior to his arrival, I could do nothing right. Anything and everything was a problem and somehow my fault. She found many other ways to criticize me during this particular time. It was often more subtle. However, after that day at the lake, it was also far more frequent and sometimes unrelenting.

To make matters worse, my son-in-law would spend 12-14 hours on his computer playing video games. My step-daughter would berate me in front of him, complaining that I was not being helpful enough, was not listening, or was doing something "deliberately" wrong. While I was used to that from her mother, I was surprised that I was getting hypocritical lectures from her while her husband was sitting there, ignoring his entire family, including his children! Despite the dramatic increase in criticism, I was at least trying to be a helpful member of the family.

Another odd thing was mine and my wife's sex life. We continued to have sex consistently. If I understand the world correctly, we even had an above-average amount of sex. However, we did not make love. It was just sex, and on the rare occasion that I tried to make love to her, it made her angry. While I was still emotionally broken from that night in Montana, I was still trying to make an effort. Of course, now I didn't have to after it annoyed her so much.

Again, my son-in-law's father came to visit. I remember it was in February because the stress before his visit was not forgettable. That month was the month she told me she wanted a divorce, but if I was willing to change, she was willing to stay married to me. I did not know what to say, so I said, "Okay." The confusing thing is that I made no effort whatsoever to change. The times I tried to change in the past met with no real appreciation. She didn't give me a metric to use to know if I was improving. After this one conversation, she never broached the subject again, which was also quite unusual.

Each month seemed to be a little worse than the previous one. I know that I started taking more overtime shifts than I had to, too. Sadly, as spring began, I began to lose my grasp on reality. What was happening should have been obvious. I saw clients go through it and even intervened to help them get to a better place. However, when you are going through it yourself, it's a different story.

There was a day at home that began with intense criticism. I began leaving the area to go to the garage and slap myself. At first, it was just one or two good firm slaps. I started to understand why my old clients did it. It was cathartic. After a month went by, the self-abuse became more serious. The criticism was not abating. So, I got in the habit of going into the garage to punish myself. I think it was the endorphin rush caused by the sudden pain. Once the endorphins kicked in, I would take a deep breath and begin to relax. It was like the world changed for the better.

In less than two months, my wife discovered my self-abuse. Interestingly, her response was anger rather than empathy. When working with self-abusing clients, empathy was critical to ending the behavior. Without an empathetic response, the behaviors would continue. Her lack of empathy was the most remarkable aspect of her response to the pain I was going through. I didn't stop, of course. Naturally, her criticism of my self-abuse didn't either. At one point, I swear it seemed like she enjoyed criticizing me for it.

Her daughter also began berating me for the self-abuse. Although she did not do it with the same intensity, she did have the same lack of empathy. I felt very alone in the home. I thought I had no friends or companionship with the people I once believed loved me.

At work, I was tasked to take care of an abusive older man. This made perfect sense; I had years of experience in taking care of this type of client. However, the company I worked for was not interested in containing his behaviors, as I was trained and expected to do in the last two places I worked. He had free reign to be both mentally and physically abusive to his staff. One day, he was yelling and criticizing me at work. After arriving home, my wife gave me the exact same behavior. I practically had an out-of-body experience. I felt the world shift, and it was like watching TV. I just stood there watching her, bewildered, and thinking that a few hours earlier, I had been treated to the same emotional attack.

Later, I would discover that this mental shift is a protective emotional response and a type of dissociative episode. The National Alliance on Mental Illness, on their website, states it this way, "Dissociative disorders are characterized by an involuntary escape from reality characterized by a disconnection between thoughts, identity, consciousness, and memory."*"Dissociative Disorders." NAMI, May 1, 2024. https://www.nami.org/learn-more/mental-health-conditions/dissociative-disorders.*

Between work and home, there was nowhere emotionally safe for me to go. I hated work and despised being at home. However, I tried to make the best of it —until I couldn't. After one more episode of berating me for abusing myself and receiving another round of harsh, unloving criticism, I figured there was no point in going on. I considered that suicide was my best option to end the cycle of abuse at home and work. I had nowhere else to go, so the graveyard seemed the best place to be. The moment I began to contemplate killing myself, I had no further need to self-abuse physically.

The constant criticism became a little bit more bearable because I meditated on what plan would be best. I don't care for pain. The most challenging part was that I had life insurance that would become null and void if it was discovered that I had committed suicide. I had two young boys that would need to be taken care of after my death. So, I carefully weighed each plan against the possibility of discovery.

My top choice was to make it look like I accidentally tried to run a train. I remember watching the busy tracks on the south side of town and concluding that I would have to time it perfectly to make it look like I was racing the train through the intersection. If they had cameras and I paused just long enough, it would look like I did it on purpose. If there were a witness, all the insurance would be lost. Then I remembered hearing how train fatalities affect the personnel conducting the train. I couldn't, in good consciousness, leave an emotional scar on someone who had nothing to do with my circumstances.

Poisoning sounded good, but how in the heck was I going to get hold of one that wasn't going to register on a toxicology screen if they autopsied my body? As my options for an accidental-looking death started to fade, I began just to feel even more hopeless. It was important that my two boys and the rest of the family living in the house had some financial options after my death, even if it was only temporary.

I hate to say this, but I even got to the point of being so angry that I thought one day, I would get hold of a pistol, go up to my wife, and just blow my brains out in front of her, as a way of getting back at her for all the crap she was giving me. I even thought about where to stand so that the bullet exiting my brain would not hit anyone else. This option was becoming extremely, extremely tempting. If I couldn't find a way to take care of the ones left behind, then I was going to damage the person who was damaging me emotionally.

That lasted until I began to think about the rest of the people living in the house. It would scar my boys and grandchildren even more. Well, that was out. I pondered increasingly silly ways of offing myself for the next few weeks. I wanted to brainstorm to see if anything would work, no matter how bizarre. I had settled on an open field east of our complex. There, at least, I would have privacy. Plus, there were no other issues or consequences to worry about.

Then, one day, I was at home struggling to think through my plan when I heard the words in my head, "Umm, you know, you could just get a divorce." I stood there, dumbfounded. For a moment, I was in shock. It seemed so obvious. Then, peace overcame me. It was like my whole world had changed. I had hope and peace for the first time in almost a year. The next day, I told a friend at work, and it felt right. I was still emotionally fragile and struggling, but hope was a powerful thing. Things remained ugly. However, now I could begin to deal with them. Never underestimate the power of hope.

My relationship with my heavenly Father began to improve steadily. It would take almost another year for that to hit its peak. Knowing that He sent His Spirit to me just to speak nine little words that changed my life is still amazing to me, even today.

Triggers

When looking up the definition of "trigger," I was struck by its origin. According to Google, it is from an old Dutch word meaning "to pull." Emotionally, you are pulling up a bad memory when you see something that reminds you of the trauma, which may cause you to react the same way you did during the traumatic moment.

I remember a very bad call when I first started working on an ambulance on an Indian Reservation in New Mexico. A whole family died in a house fire. The smell of their burned bodies stayed with me as a trigger for six weeks afterward. They smelled like charbroiled beef. Whenever I went by a restaurant that smelled of charbroiled meat, I instantly wanted to vomit. After six weeks, I no longer wanted to vomit but was still negatively affected by the smell of the food. After three months, I could eat charbroiled meat without being triggered to vomit.

To be honest, there are positive triggers. There is a field in Oklahoma where many good things happened. My grandfather took me fishing for the first time on the north side by the creek I kissed my first girlfriend. I went shooting with one of my favorite .22 rifles there, and shot off fireworks with my long-time best friend. So that field is very special and gives me good feelings when I stand in it.

However, positive triggers do not affect us as powerfully as negative ones. The reason is self-preservation. Self-preservation requires us to remember potentially damaging events more strongly so that we will survive. Whereas positive triggers do not have that direct connection to self-preservation. Positive triggers can aid in self-preservation by reminding us where we were once safe. This is why many people live in the past. The present is no longer emotionally secure, so we go to our memories to find a safe space, even if it no longer exists. When the currently unsafe present becomes even more unsafe, suicide becomes an option since the person living in the past cannot bring that past safety forward to act as a shield for today's worsening problems.

The future is the key to finding an emotionally safe place. Today's problems will not exist in the future. However, we must choose to focus on problem-solving what we face. It takes practice, especially when one of our worst triggers is a certain person who knows how to push our buttons to bring out the worst in us.

Fear and the Spirit of Fear

Fear is the actual trigger behind self-harm, sabotage, and suicide. Fear can overwhelm a person's ability to cope, and when a person cannot cope, they will seek escape. Fear is defined as being afraid of (someone or something) as likely to be dangerous, painful, or threatening. It results from believing you will be harmed or injured somehow. You become fearful when you are convinced that you will experience injury to your body, mind, reputation, finances, relationships, or some other important area of life, especially if you depend on it. Almost all higher-functioning beings make avoiding fear a top priority, and we humans are certainly no exception. I see people go to great lengths to avoid things they are afraid of, myself included.

The fear of death is generally one of the greatest fears of all. This is what makes suicide so interesting. Suicide results when the fear of an outcome becomes more significant than the fear of death. That outcome could be the loss of a relationship, a job, health, etc.

Spirits of fear play a key role in making a problem seem worse than it really is. They recruit other people to play on your fears. This is why being problem-focused makes any situation worse. It leaves out hope for a solution, which a spirit of fear counts on. It makes us blind to our options.

We have hope. *For God has not given us a spirit of fear, but of power and of love and of a sound mind – 2 Timothy 1:7* NKJV. A sound mind allows us to see our options. Power means that we have the control to use our options, and love means we have access to options that benefit others, as much as ourselves.

Triggers are also things that create fear in our minds, and for the most part, we are triggered by other people. We must watch ourselves or others during any significant life change, good or bad. Because the outcome is uncertain, which can cause emotional chaos, leading to the inability to cope. Uncertainty creates fear. Fear can create the inability to cope. Self-harm, sabotage, and suicide all stem from the inability to cope.

People who are Triggers

A lack of empathy is the source of all conflict and hurt. It is to blame for all suffering. It is what creates all suffering. You simply will not harm someone you empathize with. You can easily hurt someone in the very moment you fail to have empathy for them. Did you want to cause them harm? No. You just simply did not care.

It's also called apathy. A friend once told me that he believed that is wasn't hate, that was the opposite of love, but rather apathy. When I thought about it, I realized that hate means you still care, but your emotions are twisted. Apathy is a lack of care. You just don't care, which means you don't love. It is easier to turn hate back into love than to create love where none exists.

Disrespect is the Number One Cause of Relationship Problems

Disrespect is born out of a lack of empathy. When you don't care, you will virtually always disrespect the person you don't care about. This happens to us in relationships where we care, but the other person doesn't. They may not even mean to disrespect us, but they're not paying attention. Disrespect manifests in every area of life. Sometimes, we can ignore it, even to the point of becoming oblivious.

Take the litter on the ground. Everyone hates it, but few stop creating litter, much less pick it up. We instinctively know that littering is disrespectful. Yet, it is a widespread problem. I remember when someone who hated litter as much as I did chided me for picking up litter that did not belong to us. It shocked me. I would have expected praise instead. It was a classic "It's not my problem, so don't make it mine" scenario.

Empathy Burn Out

Empathy burn out is when a person cares to the point that it becomes too much to deal with. Then they realize that a Lack of Empathy towards the problem gives them a sense of comfort. They don't have to deal with the burden and its frustrations. Eventually, they will disrespect someone who makes them look bad because of their apathy. If you still care, don't be surprised to be emotionally abused by someone who used to care.

We all experience Empathy burn out. This is why we need to rest and refresh. Our bodies need it, and so do our minds. The problem is that occasionally, we don't get the break and become emotionally twisted. So, we end up hurting instead of healing. Why? Because our minds need to stop hurting, just like our bodies do. Apathy or a lack of empathy is how we numb the pain. The problem is that the numbness causes us to stop feeling the pain we cause others.

What do you do when living in a world of things that hurt you? You develop a tolerance for things that you don't know what to do with. We learn many of these tolerances from our parents. If we see them ignoring a problem, we assume it's okay to ignore it, too. That way, we can focus on the pains we can fix or think we can fix. If you grew up watching one parent abuse another, don't be surprised if you end up harming your spouse, even if you think you are not repeating the form of abuse you witnessed. A lack of empathy creates an emotional callous feeling in your psyche. It will come out in some way towards your spouse.

So be careful marrying a person who had an abusive parent. If they do not want to take steps to deal with what they experienced, they will likely come after you in ways you do not expect. Sadly, they will be self-justified when they do.

Bullying

Bullying takes many forms, including overt and covert. Overt bullying is what we normally think of when we think of bullying. It is open, threatening, and physical. Most importantly, it is obvious. The overt bully intimidates openly and makes no secret what they want. Most people are familiar with overt bullying.

On the other hand, the covert bully makes use of secrecy, veiled threats, and is mental. They are very subtle, and the victim is often not certain that they are being bullied. Blame is the most effective tactic of the covert bully. They want the victim to believe the bully is the victim. Mental bullying can be even more harmful long-term because the target doubts there is any actual bullying going on, and that's the way the bully wants it.

Gas-lighting

Covert bullies, especially narcissists, will use this particular tactic called Gaslighting. PsychologyToday.com author Darlene Lancer defines it this way, "Gaslighting is a malicious and hidden form of mental and emotional abuse, designed to plant seeds of self-doubt and alter your perception of reality. Like all abuse, it's based on the need for power, control, or concealment. Some people occasionally lie or use denial to avoid taking responsibility." *"How to Know If You're a Victim of Gaslighting." Psychology Today. Accessed June 20, 2024. https://www.psychologytoday.com/gb/blog/toxic-relationships/201801/how-know-if-youre-victim-gaslighting.*

Covert bullies fully believe they are justified in their actions. Convincing them that they are wrong is nearly impossible. Whereas, I've seen overt bullies come to realize their harm. I was one of those overt bullies. I regret what I did and strive never to do that again. I have never seen or heard of a covert bully changing their ways. Why? Covert bullies believe in what they are doing.

Watch for people who set you up for failure and then blame you for what happened. Accepting blame increases your susceptibility to depression and other overwhelming emotions that lead to self-harm and eventually to suicidal ideation or worse. The blame sets you up for the self-harm cycle. If you self-harm, the abuser will blame you.

All bullies use tactics to gain control over another person for their benefit. It does not matter what the benefit is. It can be anything from gaining power, influence, sex, money, and fame to a secret agenda known only to the abuser.

The Goal of Abusers

Abusers only have one goal, which is to lower your resistance to their control over you to get what they want. How they achieve their goal is varied.

However, the emotional outcome for their victims is increased fear and loss of the ability to cope with the abuse. As we've seen before, the inability to cope is what leads to self-harm, sabotage, and ultimately suicide.

How to Deal with Abusers

Leave! Find anyone you can trust and leave. Staying or going back to the abuser will only lead to self-harm, sabotage, and suicide. While it is true that occasionally, abusers do change, you can never predict who will and why, and you definitely cannot predict when. The abuser may not stop abusing you until you are dead.

If you are in an abusive job. Quit.

The purpose of abuse is to create chaos and confusion, then take advantage of the victim while their defenses are down. This tactic gains mental control over the victim, who is trusting the abuser to be normal, like them. The lack of empathy means that the abuser does not see their behavior as abuse. Abusers believe they are reacting to the victim's bad behavior. Therefore, the victim is seen as the aggressor.

When the victim self-advocates, some abusers may, at the moment, understand the problem they caused the victim. That's when they apologize and try to "fix" what happened. The relationship gets reset. Other abusers are so self-assured that the victim was wrong they are satisfied that the victim has learned their lesson that they back off. In this case, the victim does not receive a honeymoon phase. These victims learn to accept the calm without the benefits of sincere apologies or temporary improvements in behavior.

Because many victims don't want to abuse back, they will look for a way out. Sadly, just packing up and leaving is not the first thought that goes through their mind. Most stay because they can compensate emotionally by justifying the abuser's behavior, especially if they are empathic. Empathic people feel for people, which is what abusers lack. However, the abuser will push the victim to the point that when the victim fights back, the victim will begin to behave like the abuser, which increases the abuser's self-justification.

It's not usually the victimization that causes abused people to commit suicide; it's the guilt for becoming like the abuser and the sense of powerlessness combined with it. Guilt is a powerful emotion, and when someone has been hurt enough, the pain of suicide is no longer a high hurdle to overcome. Now, add conflicting emotions, and suicide seems sane compared to the insanity caused by the abuser's chaos and confusion tactics.

When a Relationship Turns Toxic

We only look at people's behavior in two ways, and it's how they also look at us. Is what they are doing good and right or not? Fundamentally speaking, these two lenses are how we view everything. We judge every single thing as either an asset or a liability. Moshe describes it as "blessings or curses." We often ask, "Is it good or bad, positive or negative, or worth my time?

Let's be sure to examine the definitions of asset and liability to make certain we are seeing them correctly. An asset is "a useful or valuable thing, person, or quality." A liability is "a person or thing whose presence or behavior is likely to cause embarrassment or put one at a disadvantage." With that in mind, let's look at how we view other people and how they view us:

One person's view of another:

Asset with liabilities= Healthy relationship
Liability with assets= Toxic relationship

We assess each person we come in contact with and make a judgment about them. We decide whether or not they are an asset or a liability. At the grocery store, the clerk checking you out will be seen as an asset if they are polite, friendly, and competent. If they do not meet your expectations, you view them as a liability. While you may forget them when you reach the car, you will remember your assessment of them the next time you see them and judge accordingly. It makes no matter if they are truly a good cashier or not. Even a bad cashier can have a good day.

We are affected by other people's opinions of us. Even if we deny it. We are just pretending. Some of us are more sensitive to other's opinions than others are. People who are prone to commit suicide due to relationship problems are affected when the individual whom they emotionally rely on begins to have a negative opinion of them. They start to see that individual's opinion of them shift from being an asset to a liability. Before they know it, they are in a toxic relationship.

When you are seen as an asset, your liabilities are overlooked, and some are accepted. This means you two can coexist harmoniously in whatever setting you find yourselves in. However, when problems arise that are not resolved, one typically will view the other as a liability, even if they love them. What keeps the relationship going is the recognition of the abilities. These assets are why the disappointed person stays in the relationship, even as it becomes emotionally toxic. Without the assets, the disappointed person would normally disengage and leave to find someone with the assets they want. However, as long as there are assets to be used, they no longer view the other person as an equal but as inferior—someone to be used instead of loved. That's when toxic emotions begin affecting the relationship especially disrespect.

Once disrespect enters a relationship, it becomes toxic because love cannot flow and flourish. The toxic person begins to slowly but surely despise the other on some level. The person who is viewed as a liability will find themselves choosing between fight or flight. Sabotage and suicide are examples of "flight." While suicide is obviously "flight," how is sabotage? Well, sabotage is not fighting back. Because, on some level, the victim is damaging the relationship to end it, not make it better. People who fight think there is something to salvage. People who sabotage don't.

Have you ever wondered why an abused partner simply does not leave the abuser? It's because they still see the abuser as an asset – believe it or not. It is when the abuser finally is recognized as a liability that the victim is ready to leave. Why do victims return? Because somehow the abuser makes themselves look like an asset again. This tricks the victim into believing that they have a chance for a healthier relationship.

Setting up for Failure

Watch for people who set you up for failure and then blame you for what went wrong. This is a mind control trick that emotional abusers often employ. They put you in a no-win situation, and when you predictably fail, they accuse you of creating the problem and being insensitive to their needs. In this type of emotional abuse, they want you to accept the blame, which increases your susceptibility to depression, thereby lowering your resistance to their future abuse. You will experience overwhelming emotions that lead to self-harm and eventual suicidal ideation, then commitment.

This blame is designed to set up the self-harm cycle. Although, the abuser rarely is looking for their victim to commit suicide. The problem is that the abuser pushes for more control until they are no longer able to see the point at which they break their victim and lose control. Think of blame as an emotional drug. Blame lets the abuser off of the hook while getting an emotional fix of control. Abuse becomes addictive.

Controlling Circumstances vs. Controlling Self

We are always looking for control. Control makes us feel safe. When we lose power, we feel vulnerable. How we gain control can make or break us. It is the difference between finding satisfaction or sabotaging ourselves.

Circumstances are events we find ourselves in, most of which are outside our control. Most circumstances are not threatening, and some are desirable—those we tend to ignore because they do not threaten us. So, we do not spend much emotional time on them. When negative circumstances are out of our control, we begin to notice where we are and what is happening.

One of the lies about good circumstances is that we feel in control. Yet, we are no more in control than when things are against us. This turnaround shatters our perception of control. Trying to control outside factors causes increased frustration, which either causes defeatism or increases control efforts. Those who grow their attempts to control can compensate for a time. However, defeatism will quickly sabotage a person's emotional ability to deal with negative events. Focusing on what you cannot control will increase your feelings of helplessness. Circumstances are not controllable forces, although they can be dealt with—just not with the idea that we somehow have control over them.

The other way to look at a circumstance we did not expect and were unprepared for is to control ourselves. That's where the power is. The circumstance may not change, but our emotional ability to deal with it increases. Why? Because we are not required to believe we are the ones to change it. However, when our focus is on ourselves, then our power is centered. Regardless of whether or not things change, we are dealing with ourselves, not the problem.

Our next focus has to be the One who can change things. Yahweh is over all things. He has actual control. Yet, even He lets go of total power to let us make our own decisions—even decisions that harm ourselves. Dealing with circumstances is a team approach. When you partner with Yahweh, you are literally taking the Chance out of your circumstances. You may not know what will happen, but you can find peace because you are not focused on the problem—you are focused on solutions.

We look to Him to calm the storm in us and flow with it. Some storms take us to better places. Other storms remove things from us that we don't need. A few storms have calmed us. By having faith in Him, we can feel hurt or sadness from unexpected changes without sabotaging. Yahweh's peace helps us deal with what we cannot change, which increases hope. Notice that the people who handle life's ups and downs the best are not focused on the problems. They are focused on their part of the solution. Remember that you are choosing between being problem-focused or problem-solving.

Process Driven vs. Outcome Driven

Process-driven people are primarily concerned with developing the ideal process, which they believe will automatically create the perfect outcome. However, they may be so focused on getting the process right that they lose sight of what the outcome was supposed to be. This means they will be satisfied if the result could be better, but the process is perfect. Process-driven people tend to be more critical, bossy, and controlling to protect the process.

Outcome-driven people are concerned primarily with the outcome rather than how the process should work. They do not focus on the details of the process. What they are looking for are the results. If the results are satisfactory, they will be satisfied with the process. Outcome-driven people tend to be more stressed, demanding, and temperamental to preserve the outcome.

In my personal experience, it is outcome-driven people tend to be the ones who commit suicide as a result of inappropriate control and criticism from process-driven people. It seems to me that many process-driven people are less concerned with the emotions of people as they protect what they deem the most important thing – how things should work. Outcome-driven people are focused on the end goal. For many of them, it is a relationship they are working on. However, it could also be affected by any other outcome that fails to materialize as planned.

Given a breakdown of what drives a person, a person will seek a solution outside of that system. So, how they are driven may be fine. What matters is the loss of control. Depending on how things spiral out of control, a person may look to sabotage or suicide to end the circumstance they find themselves in.

Who do we Sabotage

Sabotage is always against an enemy. If we sabotage ourselves, it is because we view ourselves as our enemy. The old saying goes, "We can be our worst enemies." Setting boundaries is one of the hardest things to maintain. When we are pressured by someone to do something we do not want, we may cave because saying "No" now hurts even if we know that saying "yes" will hurt worse later. Sabotage is a matter of when we choose the pain. If we are not strong enough, then we postpone pain despite the fact it is going to be harder later. We are looking forward to this moment being as easy as possible. As we get stronger and more focused, we can suffer a little now and have peace later.

Alcohol, Substance Abuse, and Suicide

"Because alcohol makes people act more impulsively, previous suicidal thoughts may evolve into action with the use of alcohol. Because alcohol inhibits the ability to reason, drunken people do not fully realize consequences and are 120 times more likely to commit suicide. Regular alcohol abuse causes depression, which is the main emotional factor in suicide. Shameful acts are performed while abusing alcohol, and these acts may lead to suicidal feelings or actions. Accidental suicide is not to be forgotten about, which includes alcohol poisoning deaths, and is extremely more likely while abusing alcohol than not. Drinking causes countless issues in people's lives, and may cause some to believe suicide to be the only option." *"Alcohol and Suicide." Alcohol Rehab Guide, January 8, 2024. https://www.alcoholrehabguide.org/ resources/dual-diagnosis/alcohol-and-suicide/*

Alcohol reduces inhibition. When someone has been contemplating suicide without acting on it, drinking, especially alone, can be what pushes them over the edge. How many shows have portrayed someone on the verge of suicide, but they don't act on it until they are intoxicated? If you are struggling with suicidal thoughts, don't drink! Get help as soon as you can make the call, especially if you are a drinker or user.

"Using data from 17 states, researchers from the Centers for Disease Control and Prevention determined that suicides accounted for 66 percent of violent deaths in 2013. About 18 percent of suicide decedents were known to have problems with alcohol, and 16 percent had problems with other substances." *Elkins, Chris. "Substance Abuse and Suicide: A Guide to Understanding the Connection and Reducing Risk." Drug Rehab, March 2, 2020. https:// www.drugrehab.com/guides/suicide-risks/*

Self-Harm

Self-harm results from chaos and confusion. Because they create feelings of unfairness. What unfairness does is create an imbalance in power or control. We perceive life in terms of fairness. If life feels fair, whether it's good or bad, we feel balanced. So if we make a mistake, then it's fair if we pay for it. However, if someone else makes a mistake and we end up paying for it, we instantly feel the unfairness of the situation. Life is inherently unfair, but there are processes to level the playing field. This is where faith, hope, and love come into play.

The longer you live, the more likely you will see that life is a cycle. When there is a down-cycle, eventually, there will be an up-cycle. The timing is the issue since knowing when life will swing up or down is almost impossible. Waiting for the upswing is very difficult when we begin to lose hope.

Why is life so unfair? Free will. For you to have free will, everyone else must be able to have it, too. It comes with consequences, both good and bad. You were given the blessing of being able to make choices, which means you have the option to help or hurt, and so does every person and spiritual entity. Chaos and confusion result from this freedom. On the other hand, order and confidence result from learning to live in the life cycle with its ups and downs. This is why we see people who can go through many problems that would emotionally drown someone else and appear unfazed by it all.

What is it that they see that others don't? They see what happens to us, happens for us. Instead of, what happens to us must be fair. When we have the attitude that things no longer must be fair but just have to be doable, the stress and fear of life's problems are not a threat. Fairness is an illusion. Free will is not. Free will means that we have choices. Choices give us power.

Yahweh is always looking at us. If we understand that things happen to us, we have the emotional power to withstand the problems that plague us all. If we stand by the concept of Fairness, we withhold from ourselves the opportunities that problems bring. He cares about us and may make things work out unpredictably—but they are worth waiting for.

It's not that there is no balance. We are required to wait for balance. Sometimes, we wait while taking care of the life before us. This is how we make faith work for us. It is putting hope into action by making love felt. Love appreciates the people around us and cares for them. Love takes the sting out of the things that sabotage us emotionally. You will still hurt, but having the faith to hope that things will get better and showing love by caring for others takes the "me" out of life. The "we" of life makes us feel a part of a community despite the problems we have or whom we have them with. That's how we have something to live for. It's outside of ourselves. Loving takes the helplessness and transfers it into helpfulness. We may have to remove the toxic person or situation to release that compassion. By looking for a way to bring light to the darkness, we return hope to our circumstances.

Our Triggers

Whatever triggers you is nothing to be ashamed of. It can be dealt with, yes, but not with shame. Somebody has been where you have been. Those who have chosen to live have faced their triggers and lived to thrive. It helps to talk to others who have walked in your shoes. They can show you what you still need to include. Think of what the Teacher says in Ecclesiastes 1:9 NKJV *That which has been is what will be, that which is done is what will be done, and there is nothing new under the sun.*

You would be surprised what the people around you have experienced. Talking about it lessens the traumatic impact over time. Professional help is a good place to start. Because of my relationship with my father, he was a big help during my healing process, as were a number of trusted friends. Find someone you trust to talk about what is happening to you.

What triggers you and why? Answering these two questions will help you on your way to healing. They provide the opening to dealing with your situation before your emotions spiral out of control. Plus, identifying your triggers gives you the ability to find solutions you did not previously think of. It takes time to wrestle with our triggers, and that is okay. Taking the time to work through them will give you more confidence than you have now.

Forgiveness

I have heard it said that forgiveness is more for us than for the person who wounded us. It allows us to move past the hurt and not keep it from becoming a trigger or reducing the circumstance's ability to trigger us entirely. A lack of forgiveness increases stress and feelings of unfairness, which can put us into an emotional downward spiral. Forgiveness negates these feelings, taking them off the table. Just because you forgive someone's behavior does not mean you cannot pray that the Father will rectify the situation. It just means that things outside of your control no longer control you. Forgiving gives you the emotional patience to wait until the Father takes care of the problem and you cannot fix yourself.

Prayer

"Dear heavenly Father, You know how I hurt and what I have been through. I trust you to see me and help me. You are the only One who knows me deep down and still loves me no matter what. I trust You and thank you for helping me throughout my life, including during this painful and challenging time. I know that you will take care of me. In Yahushua's Name, amein."

Other Realities

I began my journey into the world of pornography around the age of six when I found my dad's stash of magazines hidden in the bathroom. What I did not understand was the effect it would have on me for the rest of my life. Back then, the Internet was years away from its first tentative steps. So, finding print materials was the only option. Interestingly, print porn was readily available. I remember reading it at the grocery store without being worried that anyone but my mother would stop me. Today, pornography can go with us everywhere we go.

Depression

I don't remember when I first began to struggle with depression. I know I noticed it around age 10. I think there was a wide variety of peer-induced influences, as I went to public school from first grade onward. I lived in a struggling neighborhood consisting of trailers or mobile homes. So, I grew up knowing I was not as advantaged as the children who lived in the "regular" homes around my elementary school.

Bullying is normal, and we understand how that affects our self-perception. Being bullied was not the worst part of my childhood when it comes to why I thought suicide was an option. I did not feel like I fit in – a normal experience. However, I now think there is more to the story than simple bullying and lack of social adjustment.

"When the brain is constantly in a state of arousal, it begins to shut down its release of dopamine to protect itself from this over stimulation. Dopamine is responsible for pleasure, satisfaction, and motivation, so when it is no longer released, a person can feel moody, tired, and unmotivated, among many other symptoms. Additionally, dopamine plays a significant role in sleep patterns, motivation, learning ability, mood stability, and awareness. When dopamine is not functioning correctly, all bodily functions it affects are likely not working correctly either.

Now that we have a better idea of dopamine's role in the brain and body and how pornography affects dopamine, we can better understand the link between pornography and depression. In addition to depression, pornography addiction has also been linked to distress, anxiety, isolation, loneliness, irritability, anger, and decreased sexual satisfaction.

People tend to isolate themselves when they lack motivation and pleasure; furthermore, people often self-isolate when they watch pornography for privacy reasons or because of feelings of shame. Increased isolation can regrettably lead to loneliness and distress. Anger, irritability, and decreased sexual satisfaction are produced when the brain's reward center has become impaired due to pornography abuse. Dopamine is no longer produced, nor is the pleasurable effect commonly sought out by pornography use." *Addiction Center. "The Connection between Pornography and Depression." Addiction Center, June 13, 2024. https://www.addictioncenter.com/drugs/porn-addiction/depression/.*

To be honest, when I look back at my life, the times when I had no porn use were generally the happiest. So, for me, I think porn is a direct contributor to depression and thoughts of suicide.

Unreality

One of the worst things about pornography is its focus on unrealistic expectations. It is pure fantasy, without a shred of love. Plus, many forms of porn are highly abusive, both mentally and physically. No form of porn that I have seen promotes any type of healthy relationship. Porn over-stimulates the chemicals in the brain. This requires more significant levels of stimulation, just like chemical addictions require increasing the dosage of the drug. Because of this, normal, healthy relationships cannot be maintained. Healthy relationships do not require constant increases in the brain's chemistry to maintain "normal."

Normal relationships must adapt to the ever-changing environment. Being with a loving, married partner and exploring intimacy together is vastly superior to anything porn provides. The creativity of a real relationship will fight depression instead of causing it like porn does. In a healthy relationship, we can choose to make changes. With porn, the changes automatically come with use. It becomes a craving that must be satisfied.

The goal of porn is to flood the brain with feel-good chemicals in the same way that drugs do. This differs from what happens in a healthy relationship, which does not cause the same instantaneous reaction. When beginning a new relationship, there is a noticeable increase in the same chemicals, but it tapers off gradually and is replaced by others. This is the normal pattern. What porn hijacks is the tapering-off pattern. Relationships are complex, requiring multiple levels of interaction, feelings, and decisions. Pornography is a single, monotonous level. Maintaining this level is difficult at best. No emotion can be constantly maintained.

Healthy people navigate the constantly changing emotional landscape by understanding that it always changes. If you watch the same movie three different times, your emotional journey will be different each time. The movie never changes. What changes is our understanding, and our emotional response changes alongside.

With porn, the brain responds monotonously. However, the brain responds with less intensity as the same material is viewed. New and more intense material is required to maintain the same response. This is why I believe that porn is a cause of depression. Now, if someone is prone to depression, then porn will exacerbate the feelings of depression significantly if isolation increases.

Researchers are an Interesting Lot

In researching the information about the links to suicide and porn, I discovered a troubling trend of discontinuity. Some people don't believe that there is much of a connection. They reason that people who are already depressed use porn to find relief and then become more depressed. As they become more depressed, they become more inclined to want to commit suicide.

This may indeed be true for some people. The path to suicide takes many routes. However, they overlook the fact that porn use is rarely considered when investigating suicides. I have never seen porn use listed as a precursor to suicidal ideation in any list of reasons people think and commit suicide. Yet, it is an unappreciated cause of depression and suicide. If porn is an under-appreciated cause of depression and suicide, then should we not take it more seriously?

The Effect on Porn Stars

One of the things that I never hear anyone talk about is how the creation of porn affects the actors and actresses. I have listened to a lot of comments and cautions about porn over the years. Yet, nothing about the toll it takes on porn stars.

"Statistics on pornographic actors:
1.   The number 1 method of suicide among "porn stars" is hanging.
2.   Many porn actors commit suicide. The rate is 6X as high as the general population.
3.   Most female "porn stars" were sexually molested by adults when they were children.
4.   The pornography racket is a subset of human trafficking.
5.   The rate of Chlamydia and Gonorrhoea infection is 10X higher among porn actors.
6.   The average life expectancy of a porn actor is 36.2 years (versus 78.6 years national average).
7.   Drug and alcohol abuse is rampant, with approx—70% drug and or alcohol dependent and 90+% drug and or alcohol users.

8.   There is a high rate of mental illness among pornographic actors."
Code, Ontario. "HolinessPrompterTM." Pornography Statistics. Accessed June 18, 2024. https://holinessprompter.com/mstats.htm.

Let's look at two troubling statistics. I was shocked that porn stars commit suicide at six times the rate of the general population. That's incredible! Why are we not talking about this more? It seems perfectly obvious that this is a crisis. Does it not?!?! The other thing is that the life expectancy of porn actors is only 36.2 years. That's INSANE!! Among deaths from suicide are murder, drug overdoses, and sexually transmitted diseases. These are much higher than the general population, so they do not live even half as long as the rest of society. Do you want to support an industry that has such a high death rate?

Human Trafficking

It is known that pornography is often filmed with unwilling participants. Some of these people are under threats of intimidation, which can include threatening the lives of family members. Some individuals are from other countries who paid enormous amounts of money to escape oppression, only to become sex slaves.

According to a September 2017 report from the International Labor Organization (ILO) and Walk Free Foundation an estimated 24.9 million victims are trapped in modern-day slavery. Of these, 16 million (64%) were exploited for labor, 4.8 million (19%) were sexually exploited, and 4.1 million (17%) were exploited in state-imposed forced labor. Human trafficking does not always involve travel to the destination of exploitation: 2.2 million (14%) of victims of forced labor moved either internally or internationally, while 3.5 million (74%) of victims of sexual exploitation were living outside their country of residence. *"Human Trafficking by the Numbers." Human Rights First, October 24, 2022. https://humanrightsfirst.org/library/human-trafficking-by-the-numbers/.*

While only 19% of the global approximate 24.9 million trafficking victims are trafficked for sex, sexual exploitation earns 66% of the global profits from human trafficking. The average annual profit generated by each woman in forced sexual servitude ($100,000) is estimated to be six times more than the average profits generated by each trafficking victim worldwide ($21,800), according to the ILO. In fact, according to the Organization for Security and Cooperation in Europe (OSCE), studies show that sexual exploitation can yield a return on investment ranging from 100% to 1,000%. That's huge, and enticing to anyone looking to make bank. *Fight the New Drug. "By the Numbers: Is the Porn Industry Connected to Sex Trafficking?" By the Numbers: Is the Porn Industry Connected to Sex Trafficking?, December 15, 2022. https://fightthenewdrug.org/by-the-numbers-porn-sex-trafficking-connected/.*

Three Ways Domestic Violence Is Connected to Pornography:

* * *

1. Pornography Sets Expectations of Violence and Abuse.

Pornography fosters aggression by normalizing and depicting verbal and physical violence as enjoyable. Aggressive acts against women in pornography occur in roughly 87% of the scenes, and 95% of the time when these acts are committed, women respond with expressions of pleasure or neutrality. Pornography acts as a form of sexual education, teaching the lesson that female sexual partners ought to enjoy physical acts such as hitting, gagging, slapping, or non-consensual sex.

2. Sometimes Abusers Use Couple-Made Pornography or Nude Images to Manipulate Victims

Behaviors like threatening, isolating, gas lighting and more, are hallmarks of domestically abusive relationships. Sometimes abusers use couple-made pornography or nude images to coerce or punish victims in abusive relationships by threatening to, or actually, sharing them. The term "revenge pornography" is often not connected to domestic violence or abusive relationships, but the reality is that these phenomena often overlap.

3. Pornography Use by Domestic Abusers Can Increase the Odds of Sexual Assault

In a study of 271 battered women, it was found that 30% of the abusers reportedly used pornography. The study concluded that "the majority of women (58%) whose abusers used pornography acknowledged that the pornography had affected their abuse... Further, pornography use is linked to marital rape, which is a form of domestic abuse. Research from the journal Violence Against Women found that men who use pornography and go to strip clubs were found to engage in higher rates of sexual abuse, stalking, and marital rape than those who did not use pornography or strip clubs.

McNamara (Halverson), Haley. "Three Ways Domestic Violence Is Connected to Pornography." National Center on Sexual Exploitation, June 15, 2021. https://endsexualexploitation.org/articles/three-ways-domestic-violence-is-connected-to-pornography/.

What is the Reality

"Childhood sexual abuse has been consistently associated with suicidal behavior. We studied suicide attempt features in depressed individuals sexually abused as children. On average, sexual abuse started before age 9. It frequently coexisted with physical abuse. Suicide attempters more often had personality disorders and had endured abuse for longer, but did not differ in terms of other clinical characteristics from non-attempters. Earlier onset of sexual abuse and its duration were associated with more suicide attempts." *Lopez-Castroman, Jorge, Nadine Melhem, Boris Birmaher, Laurence Greenhill, David Kolko, Barbara Stanley, Jamie Zelazny, et al. "Early Childhood Sexual Abuse Increases Suicidal Intent." World psychiatry*

: official journal of the World Psychiatric Association (WPA), June 2013. https://www.ncbi.nlm.nih.gov/pmc/articles/PMC3683267/.

Pornography is simply a portal into a violent world. Viewing porn provides the money to keep people trapped in a world of harm both psychologically and physically. Including yourself. People die because of porn, and some victims were not even involved. It is a cycle of abuse. If we love ourselves and if we love others, we must stop the porn industry by avoiding it to the very best of our abilities.

The 100 Day Solution

When I came across an article in The Tab about Daniel Simmons, it sounded similar to my experience, since my depression was becoming more severe after regularly consuming porn. It was his solution that was the most helpful thing.

"Daniel was affected by his underlying case of depression he had since he could remember and that his addiction to porn only made it worse by numbing the pain.

In June 2013, Daniel had enough and contemplated suicide when his panic attacks and constant break-downs became too much. His voice loses it's tremble as he tells me how meditation saved him, prompting him to understand that he had a serious problem with porn.

Recognizing his problem, York grad Daniel likened it to a drug addiction. He found himself with terrifying withdrawal symptoms when he started his reboot process, abstaining from both porn and masturbation for 100 days" *Fitzpatrick, Laura. "Porn Nearly Made Me Kill Myself": York Graduate Speaks out about His Addiction." The Tab, April 30, 2015. https:// thetab.com/2015/04/30/couldnt-not-watch-porn-34954.*

Because I was an occasional user, the withdrawal symptoms for me were not so bad. Rather mild in fact. I had already taken a 5-day break from it before starting. So, the 100 Days were more liberating. However, I did experience unexpected times of cravings. I would go for weeks and then just have a craving, seemingly out of nowhere. Interestingly, accidental exposure to pornographic pictures was not as much of an issue as I expected it to be. Although, you may experience the opposite.

1. Prepare for accidental exposure
2. Take a moment to allow yourself to calm the storm
3. Remember your goals

I cannot tell you how many times I used 2 and 3. Which came in handy for other negative situations that I was also facing. Sometimes, I like to handle interpersonal conflict with humorous deflection, which can work well if done properly. However, sometimes, I could not deflect and would need to stop and think before speaking. In some cases, it was best to say nothing. By calming down first, I could better choose a plan of action.

Prayer

Maybe praying should have been number four. I hope that praying becomes a routine action for a wide variety of issues and problems. Our heavenly Father fully knows every challenge we face, and He wants to be part of the solution.

If you noticed, I did not include any Scripture verses in the above sections. Most people know that the Word does not speak well of lust or violence. However, even the secular world sees pornography as a serious problem. This is why I focused on that, rather than risk making it a simple moral judgment. When people who are not morally opposed to porn can see the damage it does, then it reinforces why we take a negative stand against it from a Scriptural standpoint without becoming "judgmental." If we don't become judgmental, then it is easier to pray without feelings of condemnation.

Let's look at it this way. Our heavenly Father passionately hates the porn industry because of the damage it does to the people He loves. He desires to rescue us from this addictive bondage and restore us, not condemn us. Therefore, we can pray with hope, not fear. I don't know what you will face when turning away from the popular addiction of pornography. You can be sure you will be better off at the end of 100 days. Praying will be a stabilizing strategy because you will encounter times of intimacy with the Father that you would have otherwise not had. This will strengthen your relationship with Him, as it did with me.

The Purpose of the 100 Days

I have heard many people give different figures on how many days it takes to begin a new habit. Normally, they say 21 to 28 days, but quitting porn is like detoxing. This means that you are not just starting a new habit but limiting an addiction at the same time. When I started my 100 Days, it wasn't as bad as Daniel's. However, as time passed, I noticed that old patterns would pop up. It would not have been successful if I had only done 28 days. In the 28 days, I would have passed the test before I would have gained the full commitment necessary for success. The little over three months of commitment builds emotional muscle, if you will. It gives you time to learn the different patterns that cause you to fail. The more intense the porn addiction, the more likely competent help will be required. It is too easy to make excuses to relapse without some type of accountability.

Social Media and Suicide

"As teens' use of social media has grown over the past decade, so too has the suicide rate among younger people, with suicide now being the second leading cause of death among those ages 10 to 34. Many have suggested that social media is driving the increased suicide risk. However, because social media is still relatively new, it's been difficult to determine its long-term effects on mental health.

In the longest study to date on social media use and suicidality, BYU research recently published in the Journal of Youth and Adolescence now offers some answers.

Through annual surveys from 2009 to 2019, researchers tracked the media use patterns and mental health of 500 teens as part of the Flourishing Families Project. They found that while social media use had little effect on boys' suicidality risk, for girls there was a tipping point. Girls who used social media for at least two to three hours per day at the beginning of the study--when they were about 13 years old--and then greatly increased their use over time were at a higher clinical risk for suicide as emerging adults.

"Research shows that girls and women in general are very relationally attuned and sensitive to interpersonal stressors, and social media is all about relationships," [BYU professor Sarah] Coyne explained. "At 13, girls are just starting to be ready to handle the darker underbelly of social media, such as FOMO (fear of missing out), constant comparisons and cyberbullying. A 13-year-old is probably not developmentally ready for three hours of social media a day."

That said, in most cases Coyne doesn't recommend parents ban teenage daughters from social media, which can backfire by leaving them poorly prepared to manage their media use as adults.

"Thirteen is not a bad age to begin social media," said Coyne, whose own 13-year-old daughter just joined TikTok. "But it should start at a really low level and should be appropriately managed.

Coyne suggests that parents limit young teens' social media time to about 20 minutes a day, maintain access to their accounts and talk with teens frequently about what they're seeing on social media. Over time, teens can gradually scale up their social media use and autonomy." *University, Brigham Young. "10-Year Study Shows Elevated Suicide Risk from EXC." Newswise, February 9, 2021. https://www.newswise.com/articles/10-year-study-shows-elevated-suicide-risk-from-excess-social-media-time-for-teen-girls.*

It seems to me that we are at a point where we need to be more critical about our views toward social media. Although, it is here to stay.

For myself, I have experienced withdrawal symptoms at times from being away from it unexpectedly. It saddens me to say that because I did not think I was vulnerable. Yet, I am addicted on some level. The way that I know that it is addictive is that it has interfered with other areas of my life. Not to mention the weird feelings in my stomach when I want my fix and can't have it. The one area I had not considered was how powerful the effect of social media is on certain people. Honestly, I think many of us don't think about it enough. So, it makes sense that it can have a powerful effect on personal image, which can affect a person's ability to handle depression and thoughts of suicide.

* * *

Is Social Media an Emotional Magnifying Glass

While I had not considered it before, my experience suggests it is. People can say anything they want without fear of meaningful retribution. It's not like the good old days when mouthing off to someone could get you surrounded by the victim's defenders when you found yourself alone. This is especially true when people fake their profiles to be somebody untraceable by normal means.

"While not all the evidence is consistent, a substantial amount of research has found associations between heavy technology use and poor mental health outcomes among adolescents and young adults. Research aside, many parents, teachers, guidance counselors and others who work with young people say social media and heavy technology use are a problem. The way young people communicate and spend their leisure time "has fundamentally changed," Jean Twenge adds. "They spend less time with their friends in person and less time sleeping, and more time on digital media." *Heid, Markham. "Depression and Suicide Rates Are Rising Sharply in Young Americans, New Report Says." Time, March 14, 2019. https://time.com/ 5550803/depression-suicide-rates-youth/.*

So, it's not just the problem of exposure to negative social media but the duration. Anything we are exposed to for several hours a day will rewire our brains. That's why we go to school for more than one hour daily. Some companies take weeks to train their employees. That is the positive outcome of rewiring someone's brain. They can gain helpful skills. Social media rarely positively rewires the brain. It can, but people rarely use it specifically for that. It's mostly just entertainment. However, for some people, it is more than entertainment; it's to gain emotional control over someone else.

"There are several specific ways that social media can increase risk for prosuicide behavior. Cyberbullying and cyber harassment, for example, are serious and prevalent problems. Cyberbullying typically refers to when a child or adolescent is intentionally and repeatedly targeted by another child or teen in the form of threats or harassments or humiliated or embarrassed by means of cellular phones or Internet technologies such as e-mail, texting, social networking sites, or instant messaging. Cyber harassment and cyber stalking typically refer to these same actions when they involve adults. A review of data collected between 2004 and 2010 via survey studies indicated that lifetime cyberbullying victimization rates ranged from 20.8% to 40.6%, and offending rates ranged from 11.5% to 20.1%.

Cyberbullying, when directly or indirectly linked to suicide, has been referred to as cyberbullicide. Hinduja and Patchin reported results from a survey given to approximately 2000 middle school children that indicated that victims of cyberbullying were almost 2 times as likely to attempt suicide than those who were not. These results also indicated that cyberbullying offenders were 1.5 times as likely to report having attempted suicide than children who were not offenders or victims of cyberbullying. Although cyberbullying cannot be identified as a sole predictor of suicide in adolescents and young adults, it can increase risk of suicide by amplifying feelings of isolation, instability, and hopelessness for those with preexisting emotional, psychological, or environmental stressors." *Luxton, David D, Jennifer D June, and Jonathan M Fairall. "Social Media and Suicide: A Public Health Perspective." American journal of public health, May 2012. https://www.ncbi.nlm.nih.gov/pmc/articles/PMC3477910/.*

Social media allows us unprecedented access to other people's lives. This means we are exposed to any form of emotional response from anyone who can comment on our pages and posts. This gives social media a place for bullies and malcontents to spit their venom.

The only advice for handling social media is good boundaries. This takes some discipline. As mentioned before, limiting the amount of time on it is a good thing, as well as limiting the access of others, who are not able to respond appropriately. Parents should be lovingly involved, which means helping with creating healthy boundaries. It should be an open, two-way conversation. There is no substitute for good conversation. Although it can be difficult, even on good days, it's worth the effort.

Any Form of Isolation Increases Suicidal Ideation

"But when someone becomes socially isolated, it's not only harmful to their mental and physical health – it's also much harder for a loved one to catch the warning signs of suicide. Social isolation and loneliness are as harmful to your health as smoking 15 cigarettes a day and are twice as harmful to physical and mental health as obesity. Loneliness is linked to adverse health consequences such as depression, sleep disturbances, cognitive decline and impaired immunity. As mentioned, social isolation is a major risk factor for suicide. The feeling of not belonging or not feeling connected to other people can be detrimentally powerful." *Monzingo, Amy. "Stay Connected: Social Isolation Is a Risk Factor for Suicide." Nebraska Methodist Health System, September 9, 2020. https://bestcare.org/news/20200909/stay-connected-social-isolation-risk-factor-suicide.*

Loneliness can be brutal. Many people find themselves unexpectedly alone, which can create unsettled feelings. We were not designed to be alone. One of the first comments about us in Scripture is, "It's not good for man to be alone." – Gen 2:18. Our Creator wanted us to be in consistent relationships. That's not to say that we could not go off and have some time by ourselves. The important thing was that there would always be someone waiting for us when we returned,

Loneliness can even hurt. I could not come up with useful examples to describe loneliness. To me, it is a special form of pain. The emptiness is uniquely unsettling. It feels like I am losing my value, my reason to live, and the purpose that I believe I have. Our relationships primarily determine our purpose in life. Our skills and talents only mean something when they mean something to someone we care about. Instinctively, we know that someone who only has a little to give to someone they care about is much better off than someone who has a lot to give to nobody.

Isolation Decreases our Value

When we feel valuable, we are unlikely to let any suicidal ideation travel through our thoughts. When our value diminishes, then the likelihood of suicidal thoughts increases. Because as our value diminishes, our self-image diminishes along with it. This increases depression and anxiety. As well as other emotions like fear, anger, betrayal, hopelessness, etc. Isolation is often used as a form of torture. Although, rarely is it used by itself. Many penal institutions still keep prisoners in isolation for a wide variety of reasons.

We were specifically designed to be social creatures. Being alone was only supposed to be occasional and voluntary. Yet, many of us find ourselves alone, quite involuntarily. This is when we become vulnerable to depressive thoughts – since we feel unwanted. The people around us validate us. Remove those people, and our validation ceases. When that happens, we feel that our emotional protection is gone. That vulnerability makes us susceptible to a wide variety of negative thoughts, including those that did not originate in our minds. The spirits of chaos can use this time to wreak havoc with our emotional framework.

The goal of chaos is to weaken our mindset and collapse the emotional framework that was previously working. Isolation prevents other people from interfering with restoring the emotional balance. This is why abusers isolate their victims. Abuse only exists when no one can intervene. So, abusers go to great lengths to isolate their victims. This even happens on a national level. Regimes that want more control begin to isolate not just individuals but entire groups. That's when atrocities occur.

It can also make us very vulnerable to having unhealthy relationships that we would otherwise not have. When we are emotionally healthy, we tend to steer away from unhealthy people. On the other hand, when we feel isolated and vulnerable, we tend to compromise in an attempt to return to a place of stability. Since we already feel emotionally compromised, we feel okay to continue on the path of compromise if it can bring some form of restoration to our emotions. Some unhealthy people are just unhealthy and simply practice unhealthy behaviors. Other people are predators, explicitly looking for someone suffering from any form of emotional imbalance. Either way, being with other emotionally unhealthy people will not restore the proper balance. Instead, they will continue to keep us off balance. Who knows what path the predator will take you down?

Solitude is not Isolation

Solitude is when you regather your thoughts and feelings to organize them and put them in perspective. We need solitude to find our emotional stability apart from other people. This is healthy isolation. One, it is voluntary, which means it is not against our will, so we are not being violated. Two, it gives us more self-control rather than sabotaging it. Therefore, we become stronger rather than weaker. It is very important that we find inner emotional control. Chaos is never far away. By practicing self-regulation through voluntary solitude, we can have greater stability when we find ourselves in involuntary isolation.

Isolation preys on our insecurities. We are not supposed to be isolated, so emotionally, we are not prepared for it. With solitude, it is a choice when to be alone and for how long. Not so with isolation because we are robbed of control over the situation. During isolation, we have to deal with the noise inside our heads—all of it, including the spiritual voices, some of which we are unprepared for. We have often been running away from things that we need to deal with emotionally. When isolation comes, no excuses exist to ignore those feelings. For some people, this can be very trying.

The heavenly Father can use these times to do business with us and get the junk out. However, many people resist dealing with Him and their junk. This leaves them vulnerable to chaos because chaos can make dark thoughts run rampant through a person's mind. Which isn't always a bad thing. Because some people get so tired of it that they finally break down and deal with it. Sadly, the chaotic noise for others leaves them so vulnerable that they desire to silence the noise in their head permanently.

Opportunity in Chaos

The spirits of chaos have only one goal: to break us down to the point of self-destruction in whatever form they take. However, what they whisper in our ears can go in any direction we choose. Whatever we hear in our minds, we can assess and examine. This is always a good thing. When we recognize a problem, we can deal with it. Sometimes, the Father lets the evil whispers stir us up to do something about things that we should have dealt with sooner.

The most important thing is to assess the accuracy of the thoughts in our heads, irrespective of the source. This is taking our thoughts captive. 2 Corinthians 2:5 says, "bringing every thought into captivity to the obedience of Messiah." This means we can control the dark thoughts when we bring them to our Savior. I know that my thought life improves when I remember Who is always with me. When I forget Him, I can think of thoughts that I am ashamed of, which I will have to take to Him anyway to find forgiveness. When we remember that Yahweh is always with us, isolation can become bearable. It won't be easy, but it is doable.

I hate feeling isolated as much as anyone. Sometimes, I have thought that it was my lot in life. However, once I realized I didn't have to be, I could empower myself to have the relationships I wanted. Sometimes, isolation is self-imposed. We don't feel worthy of companionship, so we self-isolate. Or we do so because someone made us feel unworthy. Thankfully, many people see the good in us and want to spend time with us. In this case, we can walk away from the depression and despair that someone else has put us through and reform our lives around quality people.

It is very important to be around the best people we can find. It doesn't matter why. Many times, just listening to the difference between high-quality people and mediocre people can show us two completely different worlds. By doing this one thing, we can choose the world that we really want to live in.

Breaking Isolation

Choosing wisely the people we want to associate with is a huge issue. We are products of our environment, and crafting our environment is important for our overall health, especially our mental and spiritual health. The people we spend time with will determine the trajectory of our lives. Where do you want your life to go? Once you figure that out, you can find the people going that way. The good ones will support you and show you the ropes. However, some may be hesitant if they think you are not serious. So don't be offended. They have been let down, too. Just keep moving forward. That movement is what will turn your life around. When you are with the right people, they will take notice and will be more willing to help as they see your commitment.

Commitment to Reality

Whether it be social media, porn, comic books, novels, TV shows, movies, magazines, or anything online, nothing compares to having a real life. Creating a life worth living is the best antidote to the vagaries of life. I can't tell you how many times I had the best and worst day, all on the same day. So, I learned to be very thankful for the good, especially when it came with the bad. It was my heavenly Father's blessing to give me balance to the bad by including the good on the same day. Sometimes, the bad gave me a different perspective on life and living. Occasionally, I had to learn a much-needed lesson that the good things never would. By having both, I felt loved by my Father and King. My Father wanted me to be still, and my King wanted me to deal with an issue I had not been willing to deal with maturely.

We often forget that we live in a kingdom or are so wrapped up in creating our little kingdoms that we need a reality check. Yahweh rules everything, whether we accept it or not. Our free will comes by Kingly decree.

Chaos wants us to live vicariously through fake things, inadvertently creating a fake life for ourselves. What is the goal here? It is for chaos to shatter that false life and take us mentally and spiritually captive. They hope to lead us quickly to the point of despair and death. Committing to seeing the world as it is rather than as we fantasize allows us to see both the good and the bad. It is easy to misinterpret things backward. I can't tell you how often I misread a situation because I was not focused on the realities around me and created false realities.

In our day and age, it is all too easy to create a false paradigm and then live for years in something that is fictional. That is why we have to be careful with anything that we put in front of our eyes. Many of us have really good lives, but compared to the lives we see on TV or on social media, we look poor and out of touch.

On the other hand, if we take a step back, we can see how the Father has given us more than we had the right to expect. This appreciation can lead us to greener pastures without looking at someone else's pasture. Your life is your blessing. My life is my blessing. While I may wish to have had some of your experiences, I'm so thankful for each of the ones I was given. Each of us having unique lives gives each of us the ability to spice up our relationships at different times for different reasons. In a community, we can be more for each other than alone.

Your Eyes Eat for Your Mind and Your Ears Drink for Your Thoughts

Your mental health needs to consume quality input because you nourish your brain with what you see and hear. The higher the quality, the better you will be. It is the same with food and vitamins for your body.

Reading Scripture every day is vitally important. It plugs us into the mindset of the One who created us. Even unbelievers use the truths found in it. Just not to its full advantage. Our relationship with the One who truly loves us is based on the truths found in that book. Reading Scripture and praying plugs you into the real power source. I don't know what I would do without those two things. Even today, chaos still whispers in my ear that I am not good enough and that the world does not need or even want me. My Father and the One who died for me do. The spirit of Yahweh never leaves me, even when I cannot focus because of life's pain.

Sometimes, I have randomly read a passage, and it's like receiving a text from a friend I have been talking to about my situation. So, there have been times when reading Scripture has been intimate in ways that could never be random. Find things to listen to that build you up and inspire you to create the life you want. Listening to Scripture is different than reading it. Because it hits a different part of your soul, that's why I recommend both reading and listening to Scripture, as well as other uplifting materials. It builds a different mindset than the one you had before. Life is a fight. So, we have to learn to fight in our minds first. Then, we can conquer the fights outside.

The Only Problem we Face in Life is Sabotage

Many of the real problems we face are simply different forms of sabotage. We either self-sabotage or someone else sabotages us. That's as simple as it gets. Think about this list that Messiah Yahushua gave us, "For from within, out of the heart of men, proceed evil thoughts, adulteries, fornications, murders, thefts, covetousness, wickedness, deceit, lewdness, an evil eye, blasphemy, pride, foolishness." – Mark 7:21-22 NKJV.

While this list is not all-inclusive, it covers a wide spectrum of ways we end up sabotaging each other and ourselves. Everything in that list will damage our relationships with each other and our Father in Heaven.Anything that harms someone else is a form of sabotage. Hurting someone else is not necessarily sabotaging them. A surgeon will cut a person open to remove a cancer or repair an internal bleed, and that hurts, but its life saving, not harm.

Faithful are the wounds of a friend, but the kisses of an enemy are deceitful. – Prov 27:6 KJV. Someone who loves you will tell you the truth if you do something harmful. It may hurt at first, but it's better than continuing the harm. Notice the phrase "evil eye" in that verse. Evil can also be translated as "laborious, toilsome, or malicious." How we look at the world can cause us to become weary and worn out, to the point that we can become malicious to others. This is self-sabotage.

When people sabotage us, they have a view of us that is tired and frustrated, so they believe that they are right in whatever sabotage they commit against us. Yahushua even said, "…the time is coming that whoever kills you will think that he offers God service." John 16:2b Berean Study Bible. Make sure you are not that person, neither to yourself nor to anyone else. Then, you will have the integrity to stand against the bullies who want to see you fail. The only revenge you need is your success.

Love is Setting Someone up for Success

When Yahweh created us, He gave us everything we needed to be successful, including purpose. Yahweh loves us more than everyone else combined. His love is so strong that He wants us to succeed. If the best revenge is success, what is setting other people up for success? Is it not an even better revenge? When you set up others to succeed, you prove the saboteurs wrong. You are giving yourself a better life. One that will give you both purpose and joy.

What we don't often know is that many successful people have followed this pattern:

1. Someone sabotages them, usually emotionally.
2. They continue by sabotaging themselves.
3. A crisis occurs that threatens their view of life.
4. They reevaluate their mindset and values.
5. They change their thinking to get out of the crisis.
6. They find ways to become successful.
7. When failures occur, they adapt to new solutions.
8. Then they help others to find similar success.

* * *

Honestly, this sounds like the best kind of life to have. Get knocked down, get up, and teach others to do the same. That's the loving formula for success in a chaotic world and what Scripture teaches. That is what the heavenly Father showed us through Yahushua, who was murdered and rose from the dead, to show us what He will do for us who love Him wholeheartedly. When you bring Yahweh's love into your life, you will have the spiritual and emotional strength from Him to stop self-sabotaging and love Him and yourself enough to build a life worth living and help others do the same. Love stops the sabotage and rebuilds a better life. The more we help others to set themselves up for success, the more love we show them. It feels much more rewarding to see someone you helped grow and prosper than it is to do alone.

Never underestimate the joy of your first victories. Relish them. Then, help others to do the same and relish them, too. This is the cycle of life that we were created for, and it gives us meaning. I may still be tempted by the demons of chaos with the things they used to trap me in the past, but providing hope to others gives me a reason to fight against my self-destructive behavior. When I help someone else, I feel much better about myself than most things I do for myself. So, I try to strike a balance between the things I do for myself and the things I do for others. When I find that balance, it prevents sabotage from taking root and growing into full-blow chaos.

Prayer

"Dear heavenly Father, please forgive me for bringing different things into my life that have sabotaged my life, my relationship with You, and my relationships with others. Please forgive me for the harm that I have caused others. Give me the strength and wisdom to stop sabotaging myself and others. Show me what to change and how best to change those harmful behaviors. Help me to see what to do. I ask that you show me how to be a blessing to You, myself, and the people around me. Teach me your ways and how to love You and others better. I love you because You first loved me. I know this because You rescued me from the kingdom of chaos to bring me into Your loving kingdom, where I now have a life worth living. In Yahushua's name, You are my Blessing, amein."

The Cycle and Stopping It

The six reasons people attempt suicide:
1. They're depressed
2. They're psychotic
3. They're impulsive
4. They're crying out for help
5. They have a philosophical desire to die
6. They've made a mistake

Lickerman, Alex. "The Six Reasons People Attempt Suicide." Psychology Today. Accessed June 20, 2024. https://www.psychologytoday.com/us/blog/happiness-in-world/201004/the-six-reasons-people-attempt-suicide.

The Cycle of Problem-Focusing

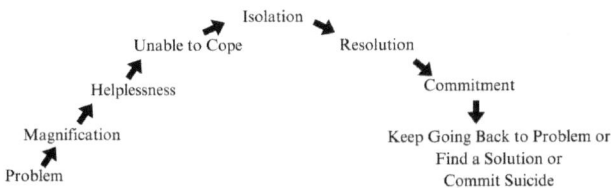

The cycle of problem-focusing begins where we expect it, with a problem that overwhelms us, often unexpectedly. When we focus on the problem, we magnify the issue as being larger than it is. As emotional beings, we usually feel before we think logically. If we don't stop to think logically, then we descend into helplessness, leaving us unable to cope. As we look around and cannot see anyone else struggling, the feeling of isolation takes a grip on us, keeping us from asking for help. It's embarrassing to ask for help when we think we are the only one weak or dumb enough to have this problem.

Once we feel that we cannot ask for help, we resolve the problem on our own and formulate a plan to deal with it. If the plan seems good, we commit to carrying it out. This is where we make one of two choices: to keep going or to end our lives, thereby ending the problem. If we keep going, we either reenter the Cycle or find another way out. Sadly, we often reenter the cycle multiple times before we decide to put an end to it. The goal of ending the cycle should be finding a solution that allows us to continue with life successfully.

I believe that the reason Dr. Lickerman put depression as the first causal problem on the list is because depression stems from an overall sense of losing control. Loss of control creates a helpless feeling that prevents us from seeking help. Depression creates the feeling that there is no help for us from anyone or that no one cares.

Loss of Control in the Cycle

Why did I not place loss of control in the cycle? I think the loss of control comes at different times in the cycle for different people. Some people struggle to control their lives before a problem exists. For them, the problem just reminds them that they do not have control. The second group loses control as the problem magnifies. To them, the problem is bigger than anything they have faced before, and now they are struggling to maintain control. As the struggle grows, so does the problem. Slipping into helplessness goes fairly quickly at this point. The third group is the more resilient. Even as the problem magnifies, they only descend into helplessness once another problem arises or the problems start stacking. For them, the additional issues cause them to lose their grip on control.

Anyone who reaches the inability to cope phase is in emotional trouble. At this point, there is no guarantee where their emotions will push them. They may stay the course, sabotage, or end it all. This is to escape the problem rather than fix it.

When facing a negative issue, it only becomes a true problem once we are unable to solve it. That doesn't automatically make it a crisis, but it is definitely a problem that must somehow be solved. If you have a flat tire, what do you have? Well, it depends on how you look at solving it. If you don't know how to change a flat tire and have no help, along with needing to be somewhere, you will probably be in a crisis. If you either know how to change the tire or have access to help, you won't be in crisis mode, even if you need to be somewhere immediately. Your stress levels will be high or even very high, but you are not in crisis mode. You may be in frustration mode; however, that is better than being in crisis mode.

Back to Problem-Focused or Problem-Solving

Problems are a part of life. Some problems can be fixed by making a call to someone you trust who can fix it. Once you know that they will take care of it, it downgrades to frustration. That's how problem-solving changes a problem emotionally. Problem-solving, while not usually easy, is empowering.

When we don't see a solution. Then, we can get fixated on the problem. This is where things fall apart. Since we are no longer focused on the solution, we are not gathering resources to fix it. Ultimately, when we don't find a solution, we must try to escape it.

Escaping problems is why we fight each other since the frustration spills out into our relationships, where we hurt each other. Or we turn to relationships that satisfy superficially but end up creating as many problems as we were trying to solve, like inappropriate sex. We may turn to drugs or alcohol. We could try dangerous activities, which may or may not be legal.

Steps to Problem-Solving

"If you don't take action, someone will do it for you. And it won't be what you want." – Author Unknown.

1. Pray and Focus
2. Identify the Actual Problem
3. Ask for Help
4. Be Open to Different Solutions
5. Find Reasons to Live
6. Make a Plan
7. Work the Solution
8. Be Ready for Unexpected Problems
9. Enjoy moving forward and solving it
10. Move On

Pray and Focus

Since we often sabotage ourselves by only moving forward during an emotional crisis, we must stop and pray. When we pray, we must focus not on the problem but on the One who can calm us and direct us. During our prayer time, we must focus on the future and our role in it. It's important to look past the problem or problems we are currently facing. Nothing stays the same. Life is a process of change. This crisis will be over at some point. Our prayer is to get on the path to a better future. We look to Yahweh for His guidance and protection.

Identify the Actual Problem

When we are in the fog of an emotional crisis, we often focus on side issues. Those side issues are often painful, but they are not the source of the problem. It can take some time focusing on what has happened to us before it becomes clear what the actual source of the problem is. The benefit of decluttering our minds is that we now have less problems to deal with. By finding the source, many other problems will either begin to go away or can be dealt with later.

When someone is bullying, the actual problem may not be the fear they cause but rather the feelings of inadequacy that we feel after the fear subsides and how we failed to deal with the bullying. Usually, it's because we did not deal with the situation in a way that left our self-respect intact. When we cower to a bully, we lose our identity and the feelings of who we thought we were. The actual problem is our internal feelings about ourselves. The bully is secondary. While the bully will need to be dealt with later, first, we need to deal with the emotions we feel about ourselves. The loss of self-respect needs to be repaired before any of the other problems can be dealt with.

Assess your self-respect. You may have had problems with self-respect for a long time or things have recently gotten out of control, and now you are struggling. Either way, your self-respect has been damaged. Dealing with your self-respect is the most important step when dealing with a life-shaking emotional crisis. This is why prayer is so important. People talk about faith and its importance in prayer. I have begun to realize that respect for Father Yahweh is even more important. When you have genuine respect for Him, then it's so much easier to have faith in Him.

Reading Scripture is very important, too. Many of the best people have had severe problems because of a lack of respect for Yahweh and themselves. Respect and love are two sides of the same coin. When you read Scripture, think about love and respect. How are people behaving? Is it with love and respect? What are the consequences when they do not have love and respect now? Yahweh loves and respects us. When we learn to love and respect Him, we can learn to love and respect ourselves and each other.

Ask for Help

Talking to someone else allows us to process safely. So find someone that you can safely talk to. You don't need someone else sabotaging you. A safe person will listen. Occasionally, as you talk, you will process through the problem without them having to offer advice. If you cannot see the solution, then as you explain the issue, they can help you find the assistance you need. If you're suicidal, call the hot-line immediately.

The benefit of asking for help is that you no longer are shouldering the problem alone. That can relieve enough stress to move forward with the emotional energy to make it out of the crisis.

Be prepared to ask until you get help. The first person we ask may not be prepared to help or be able to do so. Remember that asking for help means that you are owning it instead of being owned by it. So keep asking until you get the right help.

Be Open to Different Solutions

It's easy to get tunnel vision when dealing with a problem that causes so much hurt. Our first desire may not be the best solution. It may be our first desire because of how it will make us feel rather than how it solves the problem. Talking to someone who is not emotionally involved can clarify the situation because they may think of a different idea to make things easier in the long run. It is good to talk to different people. Having options is empowering especially after you had none. Try not to become overwhelmed if there are more offers of advice than you can deal with. Just look at the doable ones. You may be surprised who is pulling for you. Sometimes, the fact that people you don't know are rooting for you is empowering.

Find Reasons to Live

Things in life go sideways when you least expect them. When recovering from a crisis, you need internal emotional support. This is why you need to focus on the things that make living worthwhile. The best thing to do is to write them down and look at them as often as you need. Pictures are good, too. Make a list on your phone or social media. Just have it when you need it. You'll be glad you did. Don't forget to work on your reasons.

Make a Plan

To get from a bad place to a good place takes work and focus. The plan puts your efforts to good use. Otherwise, you'll be working all over the place and exhausting yourself. Your plan will also give you a road map that you will need to fall back on more than you think. There will be times when you will be distracted, stressed, or unfocused. During those times, your plan will refocus you without the effort of having to re-plan. Know your end goal and work back to the steps you need to make it happen. This approach has the side benefit of taking your mind off of your problem and onto your solution.

Work the Solution

Naturally, this is the hardest part, but after this is the reward. Focus on the goal as you work things out. There are going to be setbacks and unexpected resistance. Yet, as you gain ground, you will sense the satisfaction of learning and growing. You may have to revise your plan as you work things out because you may find out things are not working as expected. So, re-evaluate as you go. If you are still on track, then keep going. If you still need to, reassess what you need to change.

It's okay to pause, just don't quit. Sometimes, we have no choice but to take a pause. More often than not, you will not see the next step. Therefore, you have to wait until it becomes clear. It's okay to ask for help and advice. It rarely hurts to ask for help and seek advice from trustworthy people. Just keep in mind that nobody is perfect. A pause may help align things that are not ready yet.

* * *

Be Ready for Unexpected Problems

There are always unexpected problems in life. When trying to climb out of an emotional hole, there are guaranteed to be things popping up that you didn't expect. Part of the reason is that we often need more emotional capacity to see more of the field we are standing in. So, we miss things that could be easy to see otherwise. Other times, we are somewhere new and need to figure out what to expect. Just take a moment to remind yourself that things in life rarely go as expected. As long as you move forward, are willing to ask for help, and don't give up, you will succeed. It is okay to take longer than expected. You might not be ready if success comes too soon.

Enjoy Moving Forward and Solving Problems

This is one piece of advice I've never seen anyone put on a list. The truth is that we don't do hard things because they are hard. We do them because we want the satisfaction of conquering them. As you move forward and enjoy some success, take the time to relish it. Stop and soak it in. Journal it so that you can go back and relive your victories. When you finally cross the finish line, celebrate! No, seriously, you can even have a party. Just do something special to remember where you came from and what you accomplished.

Move On

Sometimes, the best healing comes when you don't realize it. Life is an adventure, whether you want it to be or not, but moving on is a choice. If you stay stuck in the past, you will sabotage your success. Look for the next thing to conquer. It doesn't even have to be a big thing. Make a plan to try four new restaurants in the next four weeks. Or tackle that thing you have been putting off, like writing a book or going back to school.

Your next phase of life is going to be new, and much of it is in your control. Now that you have conquered death's desire to destroy you, you no longer have to feel like a victim. That's a pretty awesome thing to successfully deal with. So you can take on a new challenge. Start small and work your way up.

Pray and ask the Father to show you what to do next. Pray every day about anything. Just talking to the Father relieves loneliness, especially if you are real and respectful.

Vulnerabilities

Take inventory of your current vulnerabilities. You want to know what the enemy can use against you and why. Plus, you need to be able to see where you are going to trip and fall. Everybody has vulnerabilities. Most folks try to keep them secret and pretend they don't exist. That's a setup for failure. It will

72

happen naturally, or the enemy will enjoy exposing and exploiting it.

If you know where you are weak, you can work on that, especially in your prayer time. By praying and being honest with the Father about your weaknesses, He will begin helping you overcome them if you are willing to do the work. Start with one issue that trips you up and work with Him to overcome it. As you take back control over these problems, you will gain even more courage to face life. It's not that these problems by themselves will lead you back to suicide. It's that they can sabotage your future and the successes you can have.

Think about people who fight for a living. They train with someone who can watch them and tell them where they are vulnerable so that when they face their opponent, they are less likely to be injured and more likely to win. Their opponent is going to spend a great deal of time looking for their weaknesses. The fewer weaknesses, the more successes.

It takes time to work on your vulnerabilities. You can also use the problem-solving steps to address them. Each time you strengthen a vulnerability, you gain more confidence, which makes life seem easier and more enjoyable.

Spiritual Realities

Some spiritual realities require intense focus because self-sabotage is more than a psychological issue. One day, I was listening to one of my favorite "old-time" teachers, Derek Prince, talk about a particular demon called the Strong Man. This demon is in charge of a group of demons, and as the name suggests, it is the most difficult to deal with. Derek Prince's specialty was spiritual warfare and things connected to the spirit realm. These teachings brought clarity and certainty, often missing in today's arena. The best part was that he grounded them in Scripture.

There are some realities that are way beyond the level of the mind. Psychology cannot touch them or deal with them because the spirit realm operates outside of the physical mind. When the spirit realm affects the mind, all psychology can do is ignore it and try to find a workaround, which obviously doesn't work.

The work of demons is simple – sabotage. They are good at it. I saw them destroy things in my life with ease. All they had to do was use sabotage – and nothing else.

The spirit realm is a little tricky to explain. It is best to focus on how it affects us rather than on any particular demon or angel. Scripture tells us much about how it affects us and what to do. Very little detail is given about what is happening in the invisible world. Thankfully, we get enough to help us out.

The problem with demons sabotaging us is that it doesn't make for very good horror movies. A gifted writer could turn it into a fascinating story, though. In this part, I'm only going to focus on one issue.

The Strong Man

* * *

In Derek Prince's teaching about the Strong Man, he didn't say what to do about it. The teaching had been chopped into smaller, bite-sized videos. Thankfully, it was not a problem. When it comes to praying, simple is better. I was led by the spirit of Yahweh to pray a most helpful prayer. This is the power of the Spirit to help us when we don't know what to do. I will take a different approach than he did. So, if you ever encounter his teachings, just know I didn't plagiarize them.

Then one was brought to Him who was demon-possessed, blind and mute; and He healed him so that the blind and mute man both spoke and saw. And all the multitudes were amazed and said, 'Could this be the Son of David?' Now when the Pharisees heard it they said, 'This fellow does not cast out demons except by Beelzebub the ruler of the demons.' But Jesus knew their thoughts, and said to them: 'Every kingdom divided against itself is brought to desolation, and every city or house divided against itself will not stand. If Satan casts out Satan, he is divided against himself. How then will his kingdom stand? And if I cast out demons by Beelzebub, by whom do your sons cast them out? Therefore, they shall be your judges. But if I cast out demons by the Spirit of God, surely the kingdom of God has come upon you. Or how can one enter a strong man's house and plunder his goods unless he first binds the strong man? And then he will plunder his house. He who is not with Me is against Me, and he who does not gather with Me scatters abroad. – Matt 12:22-30 NKJV.

In this passage, you and I are "the house" where the strong man dwells. Because the man at the beginning of the passage has just been set free from demonic possession, we should assume that the strong man is a demon capable or had permission to enslave the man and make him his home. Later in the chapter, Yahushua makes more references to demonic possession. *When an unclean spirit goes out of a man, he goes through dry places, seeking rest, and finds none. Then he says, 'I will return to my house from which I came.' And when he comes, he finds it empty, swept, and put in order. Then he goes and takes with him seven other spirits more wicked than himself, and they enter and dwell there; and the last state of that man is worse than the first. So shall it also be with this wicked generation."* – Matt 12:43-45 NKJV.

The strongest demon is the strongest man. Like many gangs, the strongest member drives the agenda and leads the group. When combating a gang, taking out the leader weakens the rest of the gang. Sometimes, with gangs, taking out the leader is the only thing required to put an end to their attack because the rest will scatter out of fear. On the flip side, if a gang is more cohesive, taking out the leader first will weaken them enough to finish the rest off one by one, with each one being weaker than the first. Either way, taking out the strongest one first is the best strategy. If there's only one, that's even better.

Modern psychology had no answer for this. This means that psychoanalysis will not help in the long run nor will chemicals change a person. The demon will simply try to overcome it all, often at will.

74

* * *

Where to Start

This is a little tricky. The good thing is that it is not a rigid formula. The first thing demons will do is confuse you, preventing discovery. You do not need to be possessed to have this problem. If you were possessed, it's probably more likely that the demons would not want to lose their home. So, they probably would keep you emotionally off-balanced rather than drive you to suicide. On the other hand, if they have an assignment to get rid of you, then suicide would be the easiest way because it involves fewer people and complications, which could prevent your untimely death.

What is your biggest issue that you have an unusual time controlling through normal means? This is usually the best indicator of an outside influence. Traumatic events can also cause the same problem. Although, a demon is more than capable of taking advantage of traumatic reactions. Therefore, a little caution and experimentation will help differentiate the two. In my personal experience, if I bind and rebuke what I think is a demonic influence and it goes away, then that means that it was an outside influence. If it did not go away, then it was an issue that I needed to deal with emotionally through some type of therapy or cognitive recognition.

In Matt 12:29, "binding" is used instead of "rebuking." I think this is an important distinction. Rebuking simply tells the demon to stop. In some cases, that is all that is necessary or permitted. When the attack or temptation stops, we can move forward healthily. If the demon is strong and has an assignment to torment and harass you, then rebuking will not be enough to remove it or to get it to stop. So you will need more assistance. I cannot explain why this is; I have just seen the difference in my life. There are some spiritual laws that we do not understand.

Praying is rather straightforward. So, you can have a simple or specific prayer. Yahweh knows what you are getting at, and so do the demons. An honest prayer is more effective than a "theologically sound" one. It is best to call out the demon. I call it out by the negative behavior in which it tries to get me to participate. These are things like anger, depression, lust, bitterness, hopelessness, sabotage, etc. Whatever the behavior you think the demon is creating or making worse, call it out by that name or title. That way, you can identify it, along with the problem. That has always worked for me.

Here are two that I typically use. Sometimes, I change them as they fit. If I feel that I'm simply being influenced or tempted, then I will pray something like this: Dear heavenly Father, I feel unusually depressed. Please help me with this problem. I believe that it is being caused by a demon because I don't have a reason to feel depressed. Please, take this problem away from me. If a demon is causing it, then send your Spirit to remove it from me." Then I will talk to the demon directly and say, "Yahweh rebuke you, you demon of depression and any other demons attached to me. Even Yahushua, the Son, said ... *the Lord rebuke you...*- Zech 3:2. Because He was appealing to the Father's higher authority, and if it is good enough for the Messiah, then it should be good enough for me. It has wokred every single time. The second one seems more complicated. Rebuking the strong man or the strongest demon may only temporarily fix the problem, or it may not even do that. I'm trying to understand why. It can continue its work because it allows the demon to stay in place. A prayer will look more like this: Dear heavenly Father, I feel like the strong man is confusing me, preventing me from moving forward. I need You to help me remove it. Please bind this demon in Yahushua's Name and cast it far from me. Please send your Spirit to help and protect me. Then I tell the demon, "Yahweh rebuke you, and bind you, and cast you away, in Yahushua's Name." Don't worry if it doesn't work the first time. Keep praying. If things are not resolved in the first round, I pray until it resolves. In a few rare instances, I had to pray for several days or more.

Some people will need to fast to deal with a tenacious demon. This can have more than one benefit. It will prepare you for the spiritual struggle and give you added emotional strength for other battles.

Now, you may discover that you have additional demons. As I mentioned earlier, you will want to go after them, one by one, like taking out a gang. Once one strong man is gone, the next strongest must be dealt with until they are all gone. Simply address each by the name of the problem it is causing you. Being able to deal with demons is one of the many benefits of having a loving, trusting, and obedient relationship with Yahweh. Because, as a Father, He loves us back. As a King, He fights our battles.

Prayer

"Dear heavenly Father, I come to You and offer up my hurt, pain, vulnerabilities, and life to You. You are the only one who knows everything about me and still loves me. I need You, and I want You in my life. You have my back, and You know how to help me. I am starting over again and need Your direction. Please give me Your spirit of life so that I can continue to live and have a life worth living. Thank you for everything you do that I don't see. You are amazing! In Yahushua's Name, amein."

Recovering

The recovery process begins after we have chosen to live. Living is a challenge if we believe that death is a solution to a problem. Therefore, we must firmly take death off of our emotional list of choices. Death cannot be a solution. Life is the only solution. Of course, it comes with a wide variety of options. Focus is how we change our minds about anything, so we must focus on creating a life.

So, what do we focus on now? Those are the things I have to live for. Make a list of the things you are living for. Remember goals, especially the ones you have yet to start. Focusing on living takes our mind off of death. Our minds cannot process two things at once. If you focus on the reasons you have to live, you won't be thinking about death. When you are working on your goals, your emotions follow the focus.

I would like to be able to tell you that your emotions will take over, and you will immediately feel better. In my experience, that positive feeling will only engage after some time. Our logic must be in control during this time. The emotions will fight to return to our old normal because that's what our minds were used to doing. As the logical part of our minds takes control, our focus clears from our negative fog. The list reminds us every day why we have a life worth living. The problem will likely go away once we have changed how we view it.

Putting Problem-Solving to Work

"Owning it" may be overused, but it's where we begin. Owning it is not taking the blame. Taking blame was what sent me into the spiral of depression that led me to consider suicide as my hope. Blame is when someone else wants to force you to own it for their selfish benefit. For us, owning it means taking responsibility for our life and circumstances. The hard part is owning the things that are not ours but affect our lives. This technique returns power to our lives. It is harder at first. The nice part is when you begin to realize that you have the power to change things for the better. Owning it means, "I control it. It does not control me."

* * *

Questions to ask yourself:
1. What is the real problem?
2. What am I doing to make it worse?
3. How can I make it better?
4. What is my plan to fix it?
5. What do I need to fix it with?

When you can be honest with yourself, you can begin to resolve the problem. You need to pray and admit it to the heavenly Father. This opens up spiritual resources you will need. If there are things that you did to cause it or to make it worse, owning it shows that you are ready to make the changes. It helps you face reality and understand why you need resources you haven't paid attention to before. Owning it opens doors you did not see before. Your life may take radical turns. Now, you will have the desire and the reasons to embrace the life-renewing changes. Before, you would have shied away from these changes.

One of the most difficult things to deal with is the emotional fog after coming out of a harmful emotional experience. You will feel disoriented in ways you did not expect. This is why the five questions are so important. They are designed to help reorient you back to a more normal life. It is very important to remind yourself that the real problem is not how you were treated or what you faced. The real problem is outside of you. You have the resources in your life to deal with it and move on.

After dealing with the fact that the real problem is external, you can look at it like picking up trash in the backyard. "This is not me; I don't need it." While it may take much more effort to deal with the problem, especially in an abusive relationship, it is not you that is the problem. It may be how you handle it, but that's not the same as who you are. You can change how you handle it much easier when you realize that the real you is not the problem.

The real you wants something better. You want a more meaningful life and better relationships. So, relax and feel good that the heavenly Father loves you and created the real you. The toxicity is from the enemy, and you have a right to purge it out of your life. "I can survive this and find meaning and purpose." This is a great motto to have right now.

The Emotional Cycle of Recovery

1. Care about yourself first
2. Find emotional and physical safety
3. Work to normalize
4. Remember, mourn, let go
5. Rebuild good relationships
6. Focus on future goals
7. Recognize when fear, guilt, and shame try to sabotage

Caring about Yourself First

We can slip when we don't care about ourselves because we run down our emotional batteries. People demand to be cared about, leaving us feeling like we do not have time for ourselves. This is the time to stop and be selfish.

Scripture says to love others as we love ourselves. Yet, we may find that we are trying to love others more than ourselves. This drains us, which is normal. Recharging means loving ourselves and restocking what we gave away.

Boundaries will be of the utmost importance. You have to think of yourself first for a while, and some people are not going to like it. Setting boundaries helps you to heal. People sabotage both on purpose and out of ignorance. The ones doing so out of ignorance can be dealt with by explaining what is going on and why. The ones who are malicious need to be put out of your life. If that's not possible, the stricter the boundaries, the better. They will want an explanation. Just don't expect them to accept it. While it will initially feel weird, you may be tempted to give in to some temptations. I caution against not going into some narcissistic indulgences because you will find yourself sabotaging.

Caring means taking care of what you need but have been putting off. Stop. Ask yourself, "What do I need?" You might be surprised to find that you have sabotaged yourself long before contemplating suicide. What have other people said to you? Some of them are concerned and care. It might be time to listen and follow through. Remember that you are worth it. Some people are sabotaging you because you have something they don't have. Their jealousy sabotages you both. So find your good and make it better, and it's okay to leave them behind.

Find Emotional and Physical Safety

When someone is actively sabotaging you, you need to get away from them. I understand that you may love them. Their behavior towards you is not love. You need love. Not what they are doing to hurt you. As you care about yourself, your boundaries create a safe, healing place. Some groups can take you in if you are in danger. It's okay to call the police for assistance in finding one. Even in war, soldiers are removed from the battlefield before true healing can begin.

If you are not in physical danger, you can look for what you need to escape the dire situation. It's okay to move out. The fear you feel is the hold they have over you, and it's all they have. The benefit of escaping a toxic environment is remembering there is more to life than surviving. An emotionally toxic climate is every bit as bad as a physically dangerous one. Like toxic air, getting to a healthy environment is like a breath of fresh air.

Work to Normalize

This is the challenging part. After being in an emotionally toxic environment, the healthy environment feels odd and sometimes scary. The temptation will be to return to the toxin because it was normal. The new normal can even give you physical withdrawal symptoms. That's a good sign that you are where you need to be. Although, it is pretty annoying. Normalization is a process of taking your feelings and logically walking them to a better place.

Your mind needs to stop listening to your feelings and listen to your logic. Your logic will help you move to where you want to be. As you thoughtfully walk forward, your emotions follow. How fast is hard to predict. Each day you don't give up brings you nearer to that emotional closure you want. It lessens your stress when you don't fully have closure.

Closure is up to you. It's not up to whatever and whoever brought you to consider suicide and sabotage. They may not even understand there was a severe problem and probably blame you for it. So closure may come sometime after you have been focusing on your new life.

Your new normal means closing the door on the past. That closure is up to you. This means that you have control that you didn't have before. Empowerment can feel weird, even scary odd. Remember that it is expected for you to control your own life and to do what is in your best interest. Your new standard is to improve your life first and then the lives of those around you.

Remember, Mourn, Let Go

Why do we have funerals? To remember what we lost and celebrate it. That's not always possible, but we have to let go. Funerals give us a point in time to say that it's okay to let go, even if we are not ready. When we are hurt, we must mourn, especially when it changes our lives. Mourning is processing the emotional hurt and finding a way to let it go. So take some time to remember, knowing you will move on to something better. Cry, it helps. The release from crying helps the body deal with the hurtful emotions.

Before you considered suicide, there was something positive that made you get involved. What was it? Yes, it went wrong, but that initial glint of positivity drew you in. You want that for your future, just from someone or something genuine.

Build Good Relationships

This even includes rebuilding good relationships. Building some will be an enjoyable benefit to healing and learning to love yourself if you don't have good relationships. While that may seem odd, sometimes we don't know what is good about ourselves until someone else says something loving about us. I highly recommend good, Scripture-based congregations that meet on the weekend. They can be a safe place to meet new people. More often than not, someone there has walked a mile or two in your shoes, so they empathize with what you have gone through. A few even offer programs for people who are struggling.

Suicide comes as a result of damaged relationships. Drugs, alcohol, and porn just exacerbate feelings, not improve them. Finding someone to rebuild a relationship with is a way to move forward and rebuild the emotional bonds that we thought did not exist during the crisis. Having a good relationship prevents us from returning to the despondency that made us think it was okay to no longer be around. Every person on earth is to benefit another person. That's what a relationship is—two people benefiting each other.

As you learn to love yourself, you naturally have the energy to love another. Then, be loved by another. That cycle of love is how people keep going. It's part of our design. Love is a cycle. By having healthy, loving relationships, you rebuild naturally.

Focus on Future Goals

The past haunts us. Goals can help us work around our past and bless our future. Life needs context. Goals provide that because we were designed to work towards accomplishing things and having that moment of satisfaction. Goals also take our minds off of the past. Otherwise, the past will continue to sabotage us.

Interestingly, people who truly care about us want us to succeed. Sometimes, we don't receive help because we have given the people around us nothing to rally around. Once we have goals and work on them, people get behind us. At that moment, we realize we have support; we realize that there is a reason we are still alive, and now it's a good reason. There are always forces working against us. Goals give us a reason to resist them and enjoy life.

Recognize when Fear, Guilt, and Shame try to Sabotage

As we heal, it becomes easier to see how people sabotage us. Yet, we will still have trouble seeing how we sabotage ourselves, which is how we got into trouble in the first place. To prevent ourselves from returning to sabotaging behavior, we need to recognize when sabotaging emotions come back. Fear, guilt, and shame are usually the first three emotions used against us.

The problem with fear, guilt, and shame is that they are part of our makeup. Entities and people have a way of bringing them back. Remember that sometimes your thoughts are not your own. So, you will have to put a stop to them, regardless of where they came from.

Fear, guilt, and shame are emotions that come from the past, not the present. If they are coming from the present, then stop whatever is sabotaging you. Then, you can free yourself from the emotions that wreak havoc on you and your recovery. Speak the truth first to yourself. Pray in truth. Remind yourself that you are recovering. Pray as you recover so that your connection to the Healer is not lost and you do not fall back into despair again. You do not work for despair. You work for the King of Kings, who greatly benefits those who love and honor Him. Despair is a slave master who toys with your emotions and has nothing to offer but temptations.

Find the good in your life and praise Yahweh for it. This sabotages fear, guilt, and shame. Plus, it reminds you that life is good and you are cared for, even when you don't sense it. Yahweh is constantly helping you. Giving Him some appreciation helps your relationship and your recovery. That way, you can stop thinking about the things that cause you fear, guilt, and shame and start thinking about life-affirming things. "*Finally, brethren, whatever things are true, whatever things are noble, whatever things are just, whatever things are pure, whatever things are lovely, whatever things are of good report, if there is any virtue and if there is anything praiseworthy – meditate on these things.*" – Phil 4:8 NKJV.

Your thoughts determine the trajectory of your life. It's not that fear, guilt, and shame go away. It's that you ignore them. Remember, when you listened to fear, guilt, and shame, you ignored all the positive things in your life. The only difference was the focus. The negative and the positive exist simultaneously. Since we can only focus on one at a time, we get to choose which one. There's your power.

Develop a Good Sense of Humor

Laughter being the best medicine is not just an old adage. One of my favorite video clips about our lousy world comes from the comic George Carlin. It is a brutally honest assessment told in a caustic fashion, but he makes people laugh, which makes you think without wanting to shoot the messenger. After you hear the clip about three times, you realize that nothing he says is funny. It's very painful and sad, but laughing about it makes it seem less impossible to deal with.

Laughter is a way of dealing with pain in a way that crying cannot do. Conversely, crying deals with pain in its way. When you laugh, you release endorphins that make you feel good. Yahweh gave us laughter to deal with the pain we would cause each other. Most laughter deals directly with things that hurt. So, when you laugh, you are releasing that pain. As the pain is released, fear, guilt, and shame are disarmed, and lose the power to recapture us.

Sometimes, we don't need to laugh; just be amused. It turns the negative into the positive as we improve our outlook on what hurt us. As time goes on, we can see that the people involved may not have been as malicious as we thought, or we can watch them struggle with the negative consequences of their actions.

Amusement, laughter, joking, and being silly can release that built-up tension that worsens things. It also gives us the ability to step back and deal with emotions in a non-threatening way. Once that tension is released, the circumstances become part of our past, not the present. A word of caution: Don't let your humor become a disguised way of criticizing and wounding the ones who hurt you. That will only make you vindictive and prevent healing.

Letting Things Slide

This is a hard one, and oh so necessary. It's hard for two reasons. One letting go of things that have been a problem and not solving them is counter-intuitive. We want problems solved, and we want them solved now!

The second is knowing which problems can slide and which must be dealt with. It would be easier if size mattered. Some large problems do need to be placed on the back burner because there are small problems that can quickly get out of control.

Take inventory of your life and prioritize the things you deal with. Look at the things you cannot avoid, like bills, meetings, co-workers, etc. Figure out a way to lower the stress and manage it. Once you begin to take control over the non-negotiables, you will be empowered to deal with the negotiables since those monkeys will be off your back. For the optional things, what can you let go of first? Or what do you need to let go of first? Do you really need your streaming movie service? Can you discontinue it and save money along with the hassle of another bill? It's a little thing, but one less thing is one less stressor.

What about high-maintenance friends and family? The person or situation that led to suicide or sabotage should already be dealt with by now. If not, you must deal with it now. These are your auxiliary stressors that added to the original problem's stress factor. They made things worse. They will have to go unless you have a real duty to care for them. Do they have to go permanently? Not necessarily. You can only answer that question after they are gone and you have healed some more or completely. If you can deal with them and place boundaries on them that they respect, then it's probably okay to have them back in your life.

Criticism is the hardest thing to let slide, and it's what drove you to sabotage your life before other things piled on top of you emotionally. People need to understand how critical they are. You can use this to your advantage by ignoring or deflecting it. Ask yourself, "How critical am I?" Sadly, I have had to admit that I had become just as critical as the people sabotaging me. I had to take inventory of my attitude and figure out what to do. Many victims become the next victimizers. That's one cycle we must break conscientiously because the guilt of hurting someone else is the greatest.

If a co-worker, who is not your boss takes a stab at you, like, "Why are you always late?" You can respond, "Yeah, I've already talked to the boss." You didn't have to demean yourself by letting a co-worker become your mini-boss, nor did you give them the answer they wanted. You let the issue slide. You still need to work on being on time, but your co-worker's criticism is behind you. You will probably have to let a number of things slide from a critical co-worker until you need to talk to the boss about it.

The way other drivers drive can drive us batty. That is one area that affects almost everybody. You may have to drive, but you don't have to let it get you. Try putting yourself in their driver's seat. You may find that they are doing the same as you are. In your car, you can put on upbeat music or teachings that can distract you emotionally, so you are only physically focused on driving. Remember that you cannot be in a positive and negative mood simultaneously.

Find a way to deal with normal everyday conflicts so that you don't go to bed thinking about them. Deal with them as soon as possible, then at bedtime, let yourself slide away into positive thoughts and prayers. This is a great time to end your prayers with the things you are thankful for and why. Let Yahweh know that you appreciate what He does for you every day. That's the best way to let things slide.

Confront Problems Early

At first, it will feel stressful. After a while, you will notice that you are getting better at it. Confronting problems early prevents the stress of dealing with them after they are nearly out of control. You will also notice people trusting you more. That is always a good feeling, which leads to confidence growth.

Talk to Caring and Wise People

This can be a major path to a long-lasting recovery. Caring and wise people put things in perspective. The more you are with them, the more perspective you gain. This makes life look doable in ways that you could not predict. It doesn't matter what you all talk about; just talk about anything. You can learn things that may help you later, and their confidence rubs off. In turn, you can do the same for someone else. As you talk to people who have successfully navigated the difficulties of life, your mind will process possibilities rather than fear. Listening to someone's story can give you the emotional strength that comes from gaining a new belief, even new faith.

Exercise and Sleep

When you think negatively, your mind produces chemicals that you can become addicted to, even though they are undesirable. Exercise produces chemicals that have the opposite effect. You can literally begin exercising with your brain loaded with negative chemicals, and by the time you are done working out, those positive endorphins will give you an emotional boost. After gaining a boost from physical exertion, you can springboard off that and put your mind to work to build a positive life for yourself. I've done this many times. Exercise and its release of positive chemicals have helped me deal with the many times that I have either been sabotaged or had sabotaged myself.

Working out is an excellent time to listen to positive, inspiring music, which further increases the positivity gains. I have even had workouts that, combined with good music, produced a buzz from the endorphins. You can imagine that the desire to return to negative emotions was extremely low at that point, so the physical workout also gave me an emotional boost.

Sleep does two things. First, it gives the mind rest. That alone can be enough to return to a more normal, healthy state of mind. Second, the dream state allows the brain time to process subconsciously. By returning you to a relaxed state, the tension that drives you to sabotage yourself lessens or disappears. Yahweh designs dreams to let you work things out without the emotionally draining process of dealing with them on a conscious level. I have woken up from dreams thinking, "well, that was weird" only to later realize that the dream was a creative expression of the issues I dealt with the day before. Occasionally, dreams even deal with things that happened years ago.

Having a relaxed body means that your mind is not dealing with the negative chemicals systemically. Those chemicals do not stay in the brain when we engage in negative thinking. They spread out in the body, affecting everything else. This is why negative thinking can make a sick person so much sicker than they were from the illness. It can even lead to premature death.

Read Books and Articles about People you Admire

Notice that I said "read" and did not include "watch shows" about those you admire. The reason is that watching a show does not go into the detail that reading does. The person producing the show may leave out something that would have been important to you. As you read, you can meditate on what you learn. True meditation is not clearing the mind. Clearing the mind allows demons to implant thoughts that will sabotage you later. Real meditation is the time you take to think about what you have just learned. Like any good story, most of these books will deal with problems and overcome other negative issues. Sometimes, whether the problems they solve deal directly with yours does not matter. The benefit is it naturally puts your mind into problem-solving mode.

Successful people constantly operate in problem-solving mode. It doesn't mean that they are 100% successful. Instead, they live closer to that goal than anyone in problem-focused mode. So, as you read their stories, your mind orients towards the problem-solving mindset. Reading programs your mind. As you recover, you want to retrain your mind the same way you would retrain your body in physical therapy after an injury.

The Word of Yahweh is an entire book dedicated to looking at our problems and how Yahweh offers solutions. The biggest problem in Scripture is how we betrayed Him. Then, it explains how He is going to resolve our hate-filled treachery. If He can take our horrible attitudes towards Him, turn us around, and make us loving, then would He not be an excellent resource for us?

Journaling
* * *

Writing down your thoughts and experiences can be an excellent way of dealing with your feelings. However, it can make things worse. So, you need to focus on how you will heal and move forward, as much as what happened to you. This way, you don't end up wallowing in your negativity and sabotaging yourself all over again.

Journaling is cathartic because it takes the problems out of your head and puts them on paper. That way, you can forget them and move on. Plus, you can write out the path you want to take to heal and succeed. Using this two-fold strategy in your journal, you can map the problems and focus on your solutions. Then, when you return to read your entries, they will remind you of where you were and how you worked to get out of there. This way, you become your own success story.

Praying

Praying puts you in contact with the spiritual world. So, just praying is not a guarantee of anything. You want to focus on the True King and Creator of this world and not His enemy, who was sabotaging you to begin with. You want to ensure that your prayers bring you closer to Yahweh, which builds a healthy, life-giving relationship. Yahushua told this parable: "*Two men went up to the Temple to pray, one a Pharisee and the other a tax collector. The Pharisee took his stand and prayed like this: 'Yah, I thank You that I'm not like other people – greedy, unrighteous, adulterers, or even like this tax collector. I fast twice a week; I give a tenth of everything I get.' "But the tax collector, standing far off, would not even raise his eyes to heaven, but striking his chest and saying, 'Yah, turn Your wrath from me – a sinner!' "I tell you, this one went down to his house justified rather than the other; because everyone who exalts himself will be humbled, but the one who humbles himself will be exalted.*" – Luke 18:10-14.

The best way to pray is with a thankful heart. When in doubt, begin your prayers with as many things as possible for which you are thankful. Realizing how many things Yahweh has done for you will relax you, and it will increase your trust in Him, which will reduce the trust you have in the Things that sabotaged you.

Praising Yahweh will bring you even closer to Him. Like thankfulness, praising focuses your mind on His positive attributes, many of which He embedded in us before we betrayed Him. Yet, some things only belong to Him. Acknowledging those things begins to repair the rift between us – the rift we caused. As we begin to communicate with our loving Creator, we release the good things that had been missing, leading us to believe in our own demise. This reduces our willingness to listen to those other Voices.

Reading Scripture and praying creates a communication cycle between you and Yahweh. In this way, you are bringing life into your mind and spirit instead of death. The longer you keep this cycle going, the more you heal and grow because your relationship with your Creator strengthens. That bond will make it harder for the enemy to re-sabotage you.

Loyalty is a form of love, and when you reconnect to the spirit of love, your loyalty to death will be seen for what it is – painful foolishness. Praying with a heart of love towards Yahweh helps battle those fighting to destroy you, and yet, it won't usually feel like a battle. Most of the time, it will feel like a blessed friendship. When you are friends with the king, who has the power over both life and death, your life takes on a new dimension. First is giving Him the respect due Him while learning to be open and honest in a healthy way. Second, it is important to learn who you are and what you are meant to be. That opens up a new world with you by His side. As you follow Him, He will lead you to better places despite what the enemy tries to do to you.

Time Outs

You can use these little mini-vacations to de-stress, relax, and reevaluate your situation. Remember, it's okay not to let a problem run you over. This is the time to say, "Hold on! I'll get back to you." Once, I remember hearing about the paradox of smoking cigarettes. While smoking damages the body, the time people take to relax during smoke breaks mitigates some of the damage. I'm anti-smoking so that revelation struck me. When I had a job I liked, which could also be very stressful, I would tell my co-workers, "I'm going outside to take a steam."

Walking is one of the best ways to de-stress. While getting away from the stressor, you also burn off the stress hormones churning in your body. Remember the endorphin release, especially if you turn up the intensity.

Time-outs serve to make time boundaries. It sets up the time to heal mentally without forgetting your responsibilities. That relaxation is the same as recharging your phone battery when you're not using it. So, consider it as important as the other things you care for during your day.

Establishing Relationship Boundaries

As you protect your mind and spirit, you must protect your relationships. The people who put wear and tear on you need to be marginalized, not in a mean way but in a self-protective way. Some people don't know how they affect you. Giving them boundaries can benefit both of you. Those who don't care need a reason to do so. They may not respect you, but they will respect the boundaries you enforce.

Enforcing a boundary is always difficult at first. It usually pays off and has fewer repercussions than revenge or vindictiveness. You don't have to explain yourself beyond a simple statement like, "Things are not working out, so this is what we are going to do..." If the person does not empathize, they will not care about your feelings. Therefore, your only option is keeping things short, sweet, and to the point. Otherwise, you will be the one who gets hurt.

* * *

Build Up Your Worth

There are other people in your life who see your value. The problem is that it can be hard to see that after we have been torn down. We rationalize that we were torn down because we deserved it. The truth was that someone else decided that, usually out of envy or narcissism. The nice thing is that you are actually in control of your value. Therefore, you can decide what your worth is.

Remember that Yahweh is in control of everything. He even sent His son from Heaven to die for your sins. If you are worth dying for, your life has purpose and value. To see it, make a list of the things you do well. Ask people who care about you for help. Once you realize that you are important, you will be more willing to fight for your life and the things that you were put here to do to help those in the world around you. You are a blessing; that's why the enemy attacks you. Being a blessing is your revenge.

Relapse and Trauma Bonding

This is an interesting aspect of relapsing back into sabotage and suicidal ideation. A normal relapse can come from an unexpected amount of stress that overwhelms us. When it's over, we often go back to our original emotional state. Once there, we go back to better.

A relapse from trauma bonding becomes more profound, and we may not return to our original emotional state. What is trauma bonding? As humans, we can bond with certain important people to form special emotional attachments that go deeper than normal. The first step to bonding involves a combination of needs, wants, joy, activities, and other joyous events that make a person important and special to you.

Trauma bonding is a two-step process. It begins after you have completed step one and formed a bond with this person. The second step involves small amounts of abuse that cause you to grow towards that person instead of away. If the abuse occurs before the positive bond is formed, then you will reject it because your natural desire for self-protection will kick in. After you are bonded, your instinct changes to protect them.

People who know how to trauma bond are without mercy. Their lack of pity causes them to believe that they are the victims and that what they are doing is for the best. You see the worst in them, but they don't, so they blame you. Their blame is a twisted form of self-preservation. In their mind, they are helping you when they bond with you. Trauma is a way for them to fix what is wrong with you because you went from self-preservation to friend-preservation. You allow them to "fix" you to help the relationship.

To make matters worse, the trauma bond becomes the new "normal." Even after you leave the relationship, you will have the instinct to form the same bond with someone with the same behavior pattern. Even if you are looking for the signs of a problem, you can still be fooled. People who trauma bond with others are like chameleons; they may even promise that they will be different from the last person who hurt you. It's part of the game to get you to lower their defenses.

Trauma bonding makes it challenging to move on with healthy people because you feel weird with normal people. Trauma bonders will give you the initial feeling of real worth, only to take it away from you later to use it for their own purposes, which are always for your own "good." They are looking for targets, not relationships. You are simply an opportunity. As an opportunity, you are not allowed to disappoint them, or your value decreases, which increases the abuse to convince you to return to your original value.

Suppose you have sabotaged yourself or were about to commit suicide as a result of the abuse caused by trauma bonding and got out of the relationship. In that case, you are still at risk of beginning a new abusive relationship. You need to be vigilant to find people who have no ulterior motives that would cause them to use you. This is the time to build the life you want, so surround yourself with people who help you to be better rather than take advantage of you. Think like this, "If someone I care about was going through the same thing, what would I want for them?"

Self-Compassion

The reason you sabotage yourself, possibly to the point of killing yourself, is that you lack self-compassion. As you recover, give yourself a break. I'm not talking about being lazy or not caring for things that would sabotage you differently. What I'm saying is, "Be nice to yourself." You got to this crisis because of a lack of compassion from someone else, which turned into a lack of compassion for yourself. Because of that, you thought the world around you would be better off without you, in one form or another.

Self-compassion allows you to take a deep breath, literally—it's very helpful —and say, "Self, I deserve better. I'm not going to beat myself up. It will be better, and I will be better." Saying those words to yourself will reinforce that reality. Sometimes, we do not see what is real and create an alternate reality. That distortion is the sabotage. So, by realigning ourselves back to reality, we can relax, heal, and love ourselves.

Think about it. Self-compassion means being nice to yourself as you probably are to others. If you treat others well, do the same for yourself. Then, you will be more genuine and compassionate than you already are, and you'll like yourself for it. That will bring self-respect, leading to the life you want; you'll make better decisions—decisions that will be in your own best interest. When you begin to love yourself, you will see more people who love you too.

Moving On

It is okay to move on. Sometimes, we need to stop, remember, and mourn what happened. After that, we can let go. Taking the time to remember allows us to acknowledge what happened, see it for what it is, and deliberately forgive. Forgiveness lets the pain, anger, and resentment leave our souls. Yahweh will take care of those that have wounded you. This way, you can move on, regardless of what happens.

It's okay to process alone, write it in a journal, and/or talk with a person you trust. Let them know that you are processing it to move on. That way, it's more about listening than finding solutions.

Moving on does not mean you'll forget it like it never happened. Moving on means that it does not re-injure you when you do remember. It will become part of your life's story, which you may use to help someone else. That's how you know that you have moved on.

Recovering means moving on with a life you look forward to and are willing to fight for. You make plans that you are emotionally invested in with people you enjoy being around and are eager to take on emotional challenges you would not have had before. Your recovery is your journey. It won't look like someone else's journey, and you are okay. That's the most important thing. You matter, and you now realize it.

Prayer

"Dear heavenly Father, I love You and thank You for bringing me through this painful season. You have a plan for me, and I will accept it. You knew that I needed to go through everything I went through, and I will see how you turn everything around. You were there for me in every difficulty, and You will use it for my good. You are amazing! In Yahushua's Name, amein."

Moving Forward

Moving forward will come when you are still in the recovery phase. It will be that moment when you realize that you have to put what happened behind you and now have to work on your future. It is the conscious decision to move forward into your new life.

In the last chapter, we discussed "moving on." Moving forward means going from emotionally moving on to bringing your whole being – spirit, mind, and body – into moving forward. It is putting action to the decision.

First of all, there is no denying what happened. You are not pretending that it never happened. You are creating a new life out of those events. What happened is supposed to improve you – only if you let it. It says, "This is what happened, and this is what I'm doing about it." That's true empowerment. Denying it robs you of what you learned, disempowers you, and recreates the self-harm cycle.

Since we are not denying what happened, we can continue to monitor how we are doing, access the assistance we need to grow, and help others going through the same thing. Second of all, it is about reshaping your future. You need to have a future in your head to recreate with your hands. If you cannot visualize what your future looks like, you have no road map to follow. More than likely, you'll simply end up right back where you started.

When you are accessing help or helping someone else, you will need to be able to talk about your past and how it is shaping your future. You don't want it to become a monotonous repetition where people know what you are going to say next because they've heard it so many times. It shows that you are stuck in the past and unable to move forward, and the people around you will become deaf to your plight.

When discussing your past, simply use it only when you need it. From there, you can talk about your future and what you are doing about it. That is when someone around you will be interested in being a part of that. Most people like to be involved in something positive that makes them feel like they have done something to be proud of rather than coaxed into doing something they did not want to do in the first place. On the other hand, some people will help you if you ask. It's not that they don't care. It's that they are busy and focused on other things. So, until you ask, they will keep doing what they have been doing.

Think about it: What is the best way to meet a total stranger? First, smile and say, "Hi." This grabs their attention. Second, ask a question. The human brain naturally wants to answer any questions posed to it. Notice how I started this paragraph? This is why we ask for help instead of demanding it. However, if you keep asking for help without receiving any, you may have to demand it.

When you look at the people around you, they are busy. When you talk to them, they often stop and listen. A few of those folks are glad you did. It is okay to ask for help. There's even a small group of people that like to help. Helping someone makes their day better. Just don't abuse their helpfulness. Simply use the help you receive to stand on your own two feet. Then, repay it by helping someone else. One way to know that you have moved on is to notice that you are now helping others more than hurting from the pain of your past. When you look forward to assisting someone instead of wallowing in self-pity, you have moved forward into your new life.

What Do I Need?

You are going to start with, "What do I need today and tomorrow?" I personally have found that as I prepare for today, I also keep in mind what I need to do tomorrow. In this way, I can set myself up for success. I'm not worried about tomorrow. As Yahushua said, "*Therefore do not worry about tomorrow, for tomorrow will worry about its own things. Sufficient for the day is its own trouble.*" – Matt 6:34 NKJV. Once you are in the habit of preparing for two days at a time, especially considering how things change during the day, you will have regained the strength to plan for more long-term goals. This phase is different for every person. Some will start right away, while others will need weeks or months. As you move on, you will know when you are ready to handle more. Give yourself a break and focus on what you can handle.

Cycle of Positivity

Remember to celebrate your little victories. While at it, do that for someone else when you see them accomplishing something worth mentioning. This can create a cycle of positivity. A cycle of positivity can be created in two ways. First, do something positive or helpful to someone who needs it. You don't have to say anything. When they appreciate you, you will feel positive. The cycle continues when they choose to help someone because they have a reason to pay it forward. Hopefully, it will continue onward. The second way to create a cycle of positivity is to give a sincere and appropriate compliment. Most people rarely hear compliments during their day, so genuine compliments are often appreciated. It makes both of you feel better. Hopefully, the other person will make someone else feel better by passing along a timely compliment. You can keep your cycle going by paying attention to the good that people do around you, even if you cannot tell them. You can do so in the future.

As you do for yourself, do for others. That's a good way to build your self-esteem and self-worth. Celebrate yourself, celebrate others, love yourself, love others. It's a cycle. So, find a way to celebrate positively and healthily.

King David commended Yahweh for how He created him. *I will praise You, for I am fearfully and wonderfully made; marvelous are Your works, and that my soul knows very well.* – Psalm 139: 14 NKJV. David knew his self-worth and where his worth came from. Yahweh called the first five days of creation "good." On the day that He created mankind, He called that day "*...very good...*" – Gen 1:31 NKJV. The Creator of heaven and earth thinks we are valuable, so we should understand that we have real worth.

What if you want to go somewhere out of reach for you right now? Keep your eyes open for someone who is going there and has created a fund to help them get there. Giving them money to pay for their way may help you see that you should do the same for yourself. After giving them $50, what about giving yourself $50 to achieve the same goal?

The cycle goes: help them, help yourself. That happened to me. I never considered a certain personal goal achievable, partly because someone else sabotaged me, until I started helping others because a man at work approached me about an opportunity to help others like me. After a few months of donating, I realized it was possible for me too. So, I began investing in my own goal while still helping others. I felt great! It has helped me through some dark moments that used to sabotage me.

Make Medium and Long-Range Goals

What you saw in my example of helping others first, which ended up helping me, is a good example of making a medium—to long-range goal. I went from focusing on the short term to focusing on something that could not be accomplished this year so that would be more long-term. Medium range is months to a year. Long-term is years.

As I began to think of my long-term goal, my short to medium-term goals also came into focus. I then created a series of steps to achieve my goals in the order that would be advantageous to accomplishing my long-term goal. Then, as some other long-term goals came into being, I could organize them around the original long-term goal.

As life gets in the way of our goals, we simply rearrange things to accomplish them. Sometimes, goals must be placed on the back burner, but we remember them. It's just a pause. Write down your goals. Doing that means you will remember them during unexpected pauses. When you have a break in the action, you can refocus long enough to invest back in them, whether emotionally, financially, physically, or whatnot. At least you spent some time and energy on what will fulfill your dreams. Moving an inch is better than not moving at all.

* * *

Navigating your New Life

Navigation is getting somewhere that could be more straightforward and easy. Goals tell us where we are going. Reaching those goal points requires navigating obstacles that cannot be seen beforehand. Some obstacles may be evident to you, such as someone you know will disapprove. So you can begin to tackle that in your mind before starting. However, some obstacles are wholly unpredictable. You won't see them coming, even if you brainstormed with ten other wise people. Because you will have a general idea of how to accomplish your first goal, you can use these unexpected obstacles as good practice for your more long-range and challenging goals. I don't recommend making your first goal too difficult.

Your first goal should be doable and fulfilling. You want your goal to be more than learning to cook a new recipe. If you like to cook, why not make your cookbook of favorite recipes? You don't have to publish it, just have it for yourself and maybe your loved ones. There are apps out there that can help you make it look professional and customized to your style. Plus, it would make a lovely heirloom.

Learning to navigate means more than just the physical skills involved; in the case of recovery, emotional skills are involved as well. There will be moments of blessing that come with the obstacles. It's like Heaven and Hell are racing to beat each other to help or hinder you. That's natural.

Heaven and Hell are both interested in you. This is why you must pray every day. Yahweh knows your path. While He is unlikely to lay it out for you, He will often give you the hints and help you need to navigate those obstacles the evil one uses to prevent you from succeeding. As you pray, remember who the King is and is not. Yahweh is the King, meaning His thoughts and goals take priority. You are not the king, nor is Satan nor any of his demons, who plague you. Yahweh is the absolute authority, even when He does not use it. Your priority is to come alongside Yahweh rather than be out front. As you walk with Him, He shows you how things go. This includes the disappointments that you didn't see coming.

Not all goals are good for you. You may want something, but the heavenly Father knows that it will lead you away from the good things He has in store. Sadly, because He respects our free will, He sometimes gives us the very thing He doesn't want us to have. Then, we regret it later.

I am certain that this sounds counter-intuitive, but trust has to be earned. If you don't trust Him with His plan, He will gladly show you your weaknesses. Don't ask me how I know that. So come along side of Yahweh and, if need be, go behind Him and follow. Following can simply mean waiting. Waiting is often the most challenging thing the Father asks of us. We may be given a goal from Him, but we will have to wait longer than we expected before being able to work on it. Afterward, the timing will seem perfect when it didn't beforehand.

Being constantly thankful is one of the best ways of dealing with the disappointments the obstacles bring. When the enemy wants to sabotage you, and you are instead thankful for what you have, it messes him up. Thankfulness gives Yahweh the rightly deserved appreciation for the help He gives you, even when you don't see it. Thankfulness prevents you from sabotaging yourself and your relationships. There have been times when I wanted to wallow in bitterness and frustration but let those emotions go and thanked my Father instead. It prevented me from sabotaging myself further and improved my relationship with Him, which, in turn, helped my other relationships.

Navigating Obstacles

There are three main types of obstacles. The first are tests to bring out who you are. The second is those from the enemy preventing you from reaching your goal, and the third is those that redirect you from somewhere you should not go.

In Scripture, Job contains 42 chapters dedicated to dealing with the problem of people not understanding who they are and why that's bad. Job thought he was a truly great guy. He and some of his friends had an attitude problem. It took severe trials to get Job's attention, and the attention of his friends before they were ready to listen to Yahweh correct them. If these trials had not happened, none of them would have been ready to hear what needed to be said.

Certain goals cause the enemy to attack no matter what you do – anything that blesses Yahweh and His Kingdom. Some attacks are prevented, but not all of them. Do you recognize that your goal is important enough to bring the attention of your enemies? Some of the best compliments to your character are who your enemies are. If you have the attention of those truly lacking in goodness, then you are on the right track. So keep going.

Occasionally, we have a goal in mind that may cause us to lose more than we gain. We cannot see the problem because we lack the foresight to see that the path will lead us to someplace that will not fulfill our longing or worse. It's not that the goal is wrong by itself. It's just wrong for us.

So when you hit obstacles and are having more trouble than expected, ask yourself these three questions:
1. Is there something I need to fix?
2. Does the enemy want me to stop?
3. What path am I on?

If these three questions do not help you to see the problem or how to correct it, the obstacle can be a timing issue or a lack of know-how. It may not be the right time, or you don't know how to accomplish it yet.

Some Predictable Obstacles
1. Fear of Failure

2. Disapproving friends and family
3. Sabotaging habits
4. Poor time management
5. Not planning for problems
6. Distractions
7. Not asking for help
8. Lack of faith
9. Giving up when things get hard

This is hardly a complete list, but it's a good place to start when you are working on correcting the problems coming from you. When we are our worst enemy, we have to ask the first question, specifically, "What do I need to fix?" As you move forward, take the time to look at how you sabotage yourself. When you discover how you sabotage yourself, then you can fix it. Moving on means I can ask the hard questions about myself. If I don't like what I see, I can fix it and improve my life.

The opposite of sabotage is success, or, more accurately, the willingness to do the work it takes to succeed. So many times, success comes to those who fail to give up. We may think they are extra-special when, in fact, they are average people who keep going when others quit. Victory often goes to the most determined.

Navigating Mistakes

I know that I have a hard time dealing with my mistakes. For most of my life, I have beat myself up pretty well for many of the blunders I have committed. Quite a few people have pointed that out to me. Now, I try to give myself some slack and a little grace.

One time recently, I was thinking about the possibilities of a decision that could come with some negative consequences. I talked with my sister, who made matter-of-fact comments that helped me see that I should not worry and move ahead. The benefit of discussing an issue beforehand was that it put any mistakes into perspective. I realized it might be beneficial to go the more challenging route and prepare for the challenges instead of taking the easy way. So, I accepted the fact that until everything happened, I would not know if it was a mistake or not. To have faith that my heavenly Father knew my decision. In this way, I was mentally ready to take a leap of faith that would help me grow. However, it turned out that it would be for my benefit. In this instance, I prepared to deal with a possible mistake before knowing if it was. That way, I could be emotionally ready if things went wrong. Plus, I could make some mental notes that if things did not go how I expected, I could prepare in this way or that.

After making a mistake, how do you handle the blunder? First, decide that you will no longer beat yourself up for it. Second, you are going to handle it humbly. Third, it is fixable, once you remove the crisis factor of having a lapse of good judgment, you can calmly work on repairing any damage that resulted. Have you not told someone "not to worry" when they messed up? The same goes for you.

Some blunders are worse than others, but the process is always the same. If you screw up, the consequences may be severe. You may lose important opportunities and even relationships. Yes, your life may change in ways you did not expect or want. Remember, it's not worth sabotaging or killing yourself over. You are moving from that belief system to one that says, "Life is worth living, no matter what I have done." That's where your emotional strength now comes from: "I'm going to overcome." A mistake is an accidental sabotage, not a deliberate one. So, deliberately work on cleaning the mess up and moving on.

If your life dramatically changes, think of it like a death and grieve for a time. Then, when you have accepted the loss, move on toward your new path. Don't forget that you can use your story to help others.

Prevention Strategies

Mistakes are obstacles like anything else. Yes, they are self-inflicted, but not intentionally so. As long as you are willing to deal with a mistake as an obstacle, you will be able to move forward.

Therefore, we need to ask this question, "What did I learn from this?" What you learn from navigating any obstacle is going to help you in the future. The benefit of learning from your mistakes is that you can become the better person that you desire to be.

Some questions to ask:
1. Were there warning signs I ignored?
2. Was I doing my best or slacking off?
3. Did I rush things?
4. Did I procrastinate?
5. Was I in control of my emotions?
6. Did I allow myself to sabotage it?

You may need to ask yourself other hard questions about why the mistake occurred, especially the one about sabotaging and what led up to it. If you can honestly deal with the reasons why you sabotage, then you are ready to move forward.

The Benefits of Mistakes

Honestly, some mistakes make us better. We become more focused, more determined, and more realistic. This is true of the times when other people are sabotaging us. We become stronger and more capable when we deal with them and/or the aftermath of their undermining us. It doesn't mean that we don't hurt and need to heal. It just means that we moved on from hurting ourselves. Go for your goals. You are worth it!

The Eight Things by Joe McGee
1. Strong Sense of Self-Worth
2. Great Vision
3. Keep a Budget
4. Organizational Skills
5. Humble Attitude – Be Teachable
6. Communication Skills
7. Good Character
8. Sense of Humor

I took this from a TV show I watched one day, "Faith For Families." I wrote it down on a 3x5 card and carried it everywhere I went. I hope it helps you, too. Notice that the number one thing is a strong sense of self-worth. With everything that life throws at us, that strong sense of self-worth gets us through it all. We are the pinnacle of Yahweh's creation. We are the one thing He created that He wants to spend eternity with, and He goes through a great deal of trouble to make certain He can.

That strong sense of self-worth is first because, if it isn't, none of the rest matters. If you do not think you are essential, you will not believe anything you do is important and will undermine your future. Your future is a benefit to yourself and those around you. You can be that blessing when you see and acknowledge that you are very important.

The great vision is your most important goal. It's the goal that you would really hate to die before you accomplish it. It is the one that is more pressing than the other goals. You may even lose sleep if you cannot see it through. That goal is the one you prioritize all your other goals around. It gives you a reason to live that the enemy was trying to steal from you. So, steal it back and run with it!

Don't forget to have a good laugh about the way life unfolds. If you are doing your best and are being a good person while you do it, then you have the right to stop and laugh when things go wonky. It's part of your story. Enjoy it and help others to see the humor in the wonkiness of it all. Yes, "wonkiness" is a word. It means *The state or condition of being wonky.* So, "Ha!"

Laughing gives you those feel-good chemicals. It changes the way that you remember the incident. Once you laugh at it, your brain changes it from bad to okay. Since laughter was given to us to deal with our pain, it makes us more relatable when they listen to our story.

It's okay to cry about something that hurt you first. So don't think you have to make a joke about everything. Cry first, then laugh about it later. Crying gets rid of the toxic emotional elements. Laughter replaces it with the positive emotional elements necessary for moving on healthily.

* * *

The Power of Compliments

"A compliment wields great possibility. It shows respect, admiration, approval, gratitude, trust, appreciation, and hope. One of the most generous things you can do is to give someone else a true and meaningful compliment. I encourage you to start with the next person you encounter." *Gottsman, Diane. "The Incredible Power of Compliments." The Huffington Post, June 6, 2014. http://www.huffingtonpost.com/diane-gottsman/ conscious-relationships_b_5062756.html.*

When giving a compliment, you are focusing on someone's good, which means that you are not focused on the negative. So, it can be a blessing for both of you. Your benefit comes from placing your thoughts on good things, which makes you feel better. When you make someone else feel better, you reap a two-fold harvest of positivity.

If you are not used to giving compliments, you may have to work at it. It is a valuable skill to have. It is so much better than tearing people down. The evil spirits we contend with are experts at tearing people down. So, helping someone to see their value is an excellent way of fighting evil. The one thing that makes compliments valuable is their sincerity. If you just cannot find something sincere to say, you don't have to say anything. I have seen people give compliments so freely that after a while, they lose their value.

There have been times when I wanted to give a compliment but did not know what to say. So, I took the time to see if I could give a compliment about something other than the obvious. If a cashier was struggling with my purchase, obviously complimenting them on their cashiering skills would be out of place. If they had a nice style, then I could mention that instead. By doing so, it can take the pressure off of the problems she is encountering and make it more positive for both of us.

Redirecting Toward the Positive

We may not be able to start with a compliment because of the problems that we find ourselves in with another person. This is where redirection comes in. It is a way of looking at a negative, in order to find the positive.

Think back to the struggling cashier. If you both are tense because of the problems with the transaction, you won't be able to think of a compliment. When it is over, and the tension lowers, you can always say something like, "Well, that was really hard. Thank you for getting it taken care of. I hope that's the last time it happens to you." You have acknowledged the problem and the work the cashier did to fix it. While this is not a compliment, it redirected the situation from negative to positive.

Sometimes, the only way to deal with fear is by redirecting your thoughts to the positive. Life is a risky business. We often don't see the actual risks we take every day. However, when something unfamiliar comes up, the risks we ignore are now in our faces. This is when we take the time to look at the benefits vs the drawbacks. If the positives outweigh the negatives, then it's worth the risk. Once you have determined that you can proceed, then you can handle the obstacles as they come.

Yahweh often puts us in risky situations to prove He is caring for us. Sadly, we often need Him to do this because we are not in the right place in our relationship with Him. We blame Him for it when it's our fault. This is His way of redirecting us to where we need to be. Therefore, when we are faced with a risky future, He asks us to trust Him. This means that we can put a positive spin on how He is handling the situation facing us. This is an act of faith. Faith is the positive outlook on a negative situation. It's not pie-in-the-sky thinking. It's an all-powerful Father in the sky thinking. Hugh difference.

You will need to practice redirecting your thoughts. When you drove home after a long day at work, why did you not realize the danger you were in? You were tired and distracted. That means that you could have easily been involved in an accident that left you in critical condition in the hospital. You never gave it a second thought. Why? Because you knew that a life-changing car crash was unlikely. You had already redirected your thoughts.

You must do the same with new risks you are being asked to take in your life. Yes, things could go wrong. You need to take that risk to avoid ending up worse off than you could predict. This is why we take problems and practice turning them into opportunities. That doesn't mean you know what the opportunity is, but that you are going to give it a chance.

Don't be disappointed in yourself when you get angry and upset when things go awry. Remember to redirect your thoughts as soon as you realize where you are emotionally. Anger can help us deal with problems if we channel that energy, which is redirection. If we stay angry, we will only just sabotage the process. Redirection channels that energy to make the necessary changes to make a good out of a bad thing.

'Finally, brethren, whatever things are true, whatever things are noble, whatever things are just, whatever things are pure, whatever things are lovely, whatever things are of good report, if there is any virtue and if there is anything praiseworthy – meditate on these things." – Philippians 4:8 NKJV.

Determination vs. Anger

You will have those times that anger you. What do you do to avoid falling into depression or despair after the anger subsides? The emotions that are left will determine what you do next. If you feel helpless, then the emotions of depression or despair will overwhelm you. On the other hand, if you become determined to do something about it, you will feel more empowered. You may find a life goal that turns things around for you.

Your Self-Talk
* * *

Nothing is more powerful than hearing yourself say what you will do. You can be thinking about it, but when you say it aloud, it becomes much more real. Your self-talk signals your success or failure because it is how you program your mind. When you speak, you also listen. So, what you say to yourself is who you will become. Remember that it was your self-talk that sabotaged you in the first place. You may have nearly killed yourself because of what you said to yourself. Therefore, you know the negative power of self-talk.

Now, you need to learn the positive power of self-talk. Again, it is not pie-in-the-sky stuff. It's the faith-building stuff that gives you hope. It's taking your goals and fleshing them out. As you repeat to yourself who you want to be, what you want to do, where you want to go, and what you want to fix, you make those things real. The more real they become, the more you will physically do what you want.

If you want to replace a bad habit, the worst thing to do is to say, "I'm not going to do that anymore." Why? Because your mind wants something to do. It is action-oriented. Therefore, it is better to say, "When I want to do that, I'm going to do this instead." Now, you have a path to success rather than a stop sign. It may not work initially, but it will if you keep trying. That's building a habit.

Positive and helpful self-talk is a habit, not an instinct. This means that you will have to practice until you are successful. Don't let your guard down, or the enemy will have you back to the destructive self-talk. Remember what you want each day and how you will get it.

When you find yourself engaging in negative self-talk, especially when you become upset, stop and change the narrative. Like most folks, I have a bad habit of getting irate with other drivers. One day, I realized how embarrassing that attitude was because it was so hypocritical and damaging to my ability to see other drivers as people instead of enemies. I was not loving my neighbor as I loved myself. I would see the other driver as a person who might be doing the same thing I would under the same circumstances. I would ask my heavenly Father for forgiveness for cursing someone He cared about.

Now, I still get upset at some of the dumb things I see people doing, but I can relax more and be more lenient than I used to be. This makes me happier since I have no control over the other driver anyway and never did. Remember that your self-talk today determines who you will be tomorrow.

Your Prayer Talk

Your prayer talk is just as intimate as your self-talk. You are talking to someone who already knows what is going on inside your head before you do. How you pray determines your future even more than your self-talk. In some ways, your self-talk is prayer because Yahweh can always hear you and knows your thoughts. He knows the truth about you better than you do. Therefore, prayer talk must, first and foremost, be honest. You will become His enemy if you are not real with your Creator. When you lie to yourself, you will lie to Him, and then you will resent Him when He reminds you of the truth.

The first truth is that Yahweh is the King and ruler of all. We serve Him, not the other way around. So when we pray, we ask to be put into His will. His will can bring life and good, regardless of our circumstances. Therefore, when we pray, we are engaging power—a power that we do not control. We want His Will to be done because He has information and understanding that we do not have. It is frustrating that we cannot talk to Him face to face, but someday, we will. Right now, we have to be patient and thoughtful.

Here's what James, the brother of Yahushua, said on the topic, *"Come now, you who say, 'Today or tomorrow we will go to such and such a city, spend a year there, buy and sell, and make a profit'; whereas you do not know what will happen tomorrow. For what is your life? It is even a vapor that appears for a little time and then vanishes away. Instead, you ought to say, 'If the Lord wills, we shall live and do this or that.' But now you boast in your arrogance. All such boasting is evil."* – James 4:13-16 NKJV corrected.

Our prayers and plans must be in harmony with the will of Yahweh. This requires some humility and respect. Both of those things serve us well when we use them properly. So, as you make your plans and goals, think about how the Father has been leading you. What is it that you believe that He wants from you? This is how you pray and plan. Your heavenly Father wants to give you your heart's desires, but only the ones that benefit you and His Kingdom. Otherwise, it will be causing needless pain. We may not understand it at first, but when we do, it's often too late. So, we want to prevent that.

Prayer talk is a time of connection. It brings the two of you together. Yes, your Father wants to know your requests; however, He wants to spend more time with you. That's why He's called the heavenly Father, not the spiritual request line.

Prayer is a multifaceted gem. Therefore, treat it like a time with someone special. You are talking to Someone who is the great king, a concerned parent, and a best friend. Each prayer will be directed differently and has different attributes. When He is your great king, you must be especially humble and honoring to Him, seeking His will and His desires. When you come to Him as a child, you want His protective covering and concern. As a best friend, you want to tell Him the secrets of your soul and talk with Him freely while still being respectful and honest.

Admitting your fault to Yahweh and asking His forgiveness is very important. *For if you forgive men their trespasses, your heavenly Father will also forgive you. But if you do not forgive men their trespasses, neither will your Father forgive your trespasses.* – Matt 6:14-15. So, forgive even when it is a struggle. You may have to forgive many times. The good news is that each time, it gets a little easier. You can ask for His help to forgive. I know I have had too many times. Just be real and be loving. It's okay to vent as long as you don't forget to be respectful. Say how you feel, and if you realize you are being harsh and critical, step back, think about His feelings, and apologize. Then, rephrase and talk about how to resolve the issue with Him, not against Him or worse, without Him. Yahweh cares more about you than you do for Him, and He still loves you deeply.

The Hardest Questions

Is Yahweh my life? Or is He just simply a part of my life? Yahweh is the life-giver, but that does not mean that He is your life. Many believers are content to live with Yahweh as a part of their lives, like family and work. Only a few have Him as their life. The best people in the Scriptures have Yahweh as their life rather than just a piece of it. They often fail in those moments where He becomes only a piece, and something else also steps in. For the most part, they live with Him as an intimate part of their core being.

Having Yahweh as a core part of your being means to be aware of Him as you are aware of yourself, which is more than family, friends, or duty. It's like you recognize that He is right beside you, even when you are not cognizant of Him in the moment.

If this sounds bizarre or a bit much, remember how you were with the spirit of death and sabotage before you chose life. Death and sabotage were your constant companions with whom you shared intimate thoughts and moments. You almost preferred to be with them for all of eternity. It is only a subtle version of Pennywise in Stephen King's "It."

Yahweh is not like the It. He is love. Yet, we sometimes forget that love requires justice and discipline, making us believe He is harsh. Justice and discipline exist to counter hate and chaos. So, love sometimes has to be harsh, or if it is weak, it will let the enemy win. Love resists evil, including the evil inside you that you haven't recognized.

Making Yahweh your life is becoming symbiotic with Him. He does not take over your thinking. Instead, you are thinking about Him like He is physically with you. You are interested in what He thinks, in what He wants, in where He is going.

What you do now reflects that you know He is right with you. You are together in the good, the bad, the weird, and the whatever. This walk, for me at least, began in the surreal. It is like the Twilight Zone but where the best person in the world is always with you in spirit.

I suppose it feels surreal after feeling alone for so many years. That loneliness came from the fact that I thought that Yahweh was disconnected from me and that only praying brought that connection for a moment. I suppose that the surreal nature is due to the fact that I no longer feel that kind of loneliness. I'm walking with Him, even when I don't want to be. It helps, but I know I can't just be a selfish jerk like I sometimes want to be, and sadly, I still can be.

It is a choice to walk this way, and I can stop anytime I want. I know the enemy tries to get me to walk away from Him. Yet, I have the power to choose to walk this way. I walked with the ones who hated me and tried to destroy me. So now I prefer to walk with the One who loves me and gives me life.

Most people choose to keep an emotional distance from Yahweh, even the ones that love Him. Why? Because most people don't know the difference and can't see it in others. It's a blindness. The enemy cannot stop you from having a relationship with Him, but they can convince you to keep some space between the two of you, and it works. You have Him when you need Him while still having some "privacy" and alone time from Him.

Privacy and alone time are necessary for human relationships. It does not exist for Yahweh. He is everywhere and knows everything. Therefore, to have that intimacy of a closer than humanly possible relationship with Yahweh means recognizing that He is always there anyway and wanting it. You will engage with Him on a deeper level and talk with Him constantly. It's in the alone time that you can draw your strength from Him and become more who you are meant to be. In alone time, you read His word, learn who He is, and what He wants from you. *For the word of God is living and powerful, and sharper than any two-edged sword, piercing even the division of soul and spirit, and of joints and marrow, and is a discerner of the thoughts and intents of the heart.* — Hebrews 4:12 NKJV. This means that His word can cut through the garbage of your life and circumstances if you apply it according to His purposes and not your own.

When you put Yahweh first in your life, you tap into His being. If you are just using Him to better yourself, His word will cut backward, as it is two-edged. The Word will cut you. That's why Scripture says, *You shall love the Lord your God with all your heart, with all your soul, and with all your strength.* — Deut 6:5 NKJV. He has given to you freely. Love returns.

Fasting

Well now, this is not a normal recommendation for people who live in well fed areas of the earth, especially America. Yet, food has a powerful effect on us – so does not eating. Scripture talks quite a bit about fasting. One Internet search mentioned "40 verses about fasting" right off the top. It is not inconsequential. Most religions incorporate fasting for different reasons and in different rituals. Why? Because it works, even for non-believers in Yahweh or His word.

The flesh, as Scripture calls the body, its also another way of saying, "Our lowest being." The lowest part of ourselves is only concerned with rudimentary things like food, water, sex, sleep, temperature, etc. While important, we are so much more than physical beings with physical cravings. Our bodies are connected to our spirit through our mind; however, whichever process is dominant will control the mind. Therefore, fasting aims to make the spirit dominate the mind and quiet the flesh.

By going without food for a period, the mind begins to rely more on the spirit nature than the physical nature. As our spirit asserts more control, we become more open to listening to the spirit realm. As I mentioned before, most religions practice fasting. Consequently, we must be careful what spirit or spirits we listen to as we fast because we may inadvertently listen to someone who takes us off the path of life. Fasting gives us the power to restrain our fleshly passions, which can bring much-needed calm when experiencing chaos. As we ignore our physical nature, our spiritual nature can respond more clearly and peacefully. This is important when facing any self-sabotaging situation, especially when the chaos of death is swirling about your mind.

Meditation, Prayer, and Fasting

In Scripture, meditation is ruminating on the Word. In essence, chewing on what you read. You read it. Then, you ponder its meaning. This is best done with the Spirit of Yahweh because the Spirit was actively involved in getting the written Word preserved and brought to us. Therefore, inviting the Spirit to be intimately involved in your spiritual and mental relationship with the Word is critical to understanding it. Because what you do comes directly from who you are. You need the Word and the Spirit to make you into the person you were meant to be.

When you think about the Word and how it affects your life, you want the Spirit to guide you to where you are supposed to go. Most of the time, we are not where we are supposed to be, and then we wonder why we feel alone. Talking to Yahweh about His Word will allow you to be where He wants you to be. The primary focus of Scripture is to help us be who we are supposed to be.

Interestingly, most people make the Word a to-do book. If we focus on being who we are supposed to be, we will begin to do what we are supposed to do. However, the reverse is not valid. By focusing on doing what we are supposed to, we may be moved to be someone we were not meant to be while not understanding why. It is the cart before the horse scenario. If you have ever driven a trailer backward, you know that you can accidentally turn too quickly and jackknife, potentially causing quite a bit of damage. Jackknifing is almost impossible if you are going forward in the same direction.

By focusing on who we are supposed to be, we can avoid a wide range of problems with our identity being manipulated. Meditating on the Word, praying, and fasting with the Spirit align us with the Creator of our lives. Therefore, spending time getting into alignment with the Yahweh will bring the rest of our lives into proper alignment, which will lead to the successes and satisfaction that we have been missing.

Instead of asking questions during your prayer time, like, "What should I do next?" It is better to ask, "What do You want me to be in You?" Not only are we removing any notion of being a victim, but we are allowing the One who loves us the most to be in control. In this way, we are partnering with Yahweh against the forces of death and sabotage.

Think about it. The reason Yahushua died on the cross was because who we were being was treacherous, traitorous, back-stabbing, and unloving; even when we were trying to do many good things. By dying for us, He made it possible for us to be a new and better creation; even when we sometimes do bad things. See how the reverse is so much better? Yahushua's death on the cross did what is impossible for us to do. It was to make us become innocent, by becoming guilty for us, then taking our punishment. Notice that being trumps doing. You can do 100,000 good things, but the one time you betray your King, you are guilty of treason and condemned to death because doing never overcomes our state of being.

Let me give you a powerful example of the difference between being and doing, from Matthew 7:21-23 NKJV – *"Not everyone who says to Me, 'Lord, Lord' shall enter the kingdom of heaven, but he who does the will of My Father in heaven. Many who say to Me in that day, 'Lord, Lord, have we not prophesied in Your name, cast out demons in Your name, and done many wonders in Your name?' And then I will declare to them, 'I never knew you; depart from Me, you who practice lawlessness!'"*

The people who love Yahweh – Father, Son, and Spirit – simply are being who they are as they live their lives. Thereby doing what is in their nature to do. Those who only love themselves do what they think will help themselves out because being selfish is in their nature. Therefore, they do something to get something instead of being then doing. Because they only want something for themselves, they do what they think will help them get what they want. Yahweh the Son sees through their charade and sees their false behavior, which He rightly rejects.

Meditating, praying, and fasting allow us to be with Him and in Him, to be what we are supposed to be because of Him. It is how we have a symbiotic relationship with Him. This will make your journey of life triumph over death because you will be in Him, protected by Him—just like being placed in the eye of a hurricane. Who you are in Yahweh is always the predictor of your future life and success.

Avoiding the "I" Trap

The most powerful way we re-sabotage ourselves is to think about ourselves more than we ought. We were created for relationships, which means that most of our time is to be spent outside of ourselves in the company of others.

When Adam was created, the first person he talked to was Yahweh. He was given a task and afterward was given another person to talk to, his wife. Our first experiences are with people. So, we have to make it a priority to make time for Yahweh.

Once we reconnect with our Creator, we can reformat our relationships with people and learn to have healthy relationships. The way to have healthy relationships is to be protective. We live in an emotionally dangerous world where our next enemy may be the one who says they are our best friend. That's why we start loving the One who loved us before birth.

Then, we love as we love ourselves. Here is where the enemy lays the "I" trap. The enemy wants us to love ourselves above all else. So, they convince us to love ourselves truly but in a way that only benefits us, even if it pretends to love others. The way to love ourselves is to recognize what we need versus what we want. We may want things that are not good for us. Some of our wants come out of our needs. A want for the sake of want is usually unhealthy, but a want that comes out of a need can be more fulfilling.

The "I" Trap is laid out of our desires. Satan came to Adam and Eve and gave them the desire to be equal to Yahweh. What need did that fulfill? Before that, Yahweh gave them four things to do that addressed the real needs of their heart. He gave them purpose and companionship. The evil one gave them a craving for power that they did not need and had no purpose. Most of our answers lie in purpose and companionship. We also want things that tickle our fancy. To avoid the "I" Trap, ask yourself, "Is this just for me?"

Disappointments usually indicate a desire for something that is only for ourselves. We may not have seen it that way beforehand, but afterward, we can stop and say, "Yep, that was really just for me." Selfishness is not love. Love asks, "What is best for me and those around me?" Sometimes, we don't like the answer, but the reality is different. It's when we embrace reality that we grow and become satisfied.

Another problem with the "I" trap is that once we are caught in its grip, we rationalize that this is how things should be. We can even become so self-absorbed that we despise those who try to help us escape. This form of self-love is called narcissism. Unhealthy love causes people to twist love until it hurts instead of helps. Some victims of narcissism become narcissists and continue the cycle of hurt. That is the end goal of the "I" trap. It is to focus on self until it hurts.

Loving others means loving yourself and them at the same time. It's a tricky balance, to be sure. If you see someone who is sickly and you know that it's primarily because they eat junk and do not exercise, do you do what they do? Or do you eat better and move more? Someone in the same sinking boat is not the right person to ask for help, unless you are going to work together to solve the problem in the right way. In one way, how you would want someone else to succeed is also what you should be doing. If you tell someone else how to succeed but don't take your advice, you are not loving yourself. If you help others and leave yourself empty, that is not self-love. So, it's sobering when I hear someone tell me to do what I advised someone else to do.

Not Beating Yourself Up

It's easy to fall into the "I" trap. I was learning how to drive a semi-truck and had to back it up in a 90-degree turn. For some reason, on the second day, my technique fell apart. I was trying to do it a certain way instead of being flexible. I found myself getting more frustrated and prideful. I was determined to get it down. As I began to have more difficulty, I was less able to do the maneuver. I finally gave up and went home.

At home, my frustration turned to something else, and I reveled in something I was aiming to quit. This left me feeling empty. I had a choice; I could beat myself up or pray and ask forgiveness. I chose the latter. Afterward, I began to relax and move on to some life-affirming activities. In the end, I had a pleasant evening and went to bed relaxed.

The "I" trap cuts both ways. It can cause overindulgence or self-punishment. When we focus only on "me," we can miss some of the ways that things are designed to benefit us when things don't go our way.

"We" Focused

When emotions rise, logic drops. So, it can be good to step back and look at the whole picture—or at least a more significant piece than we are seeing. When we feel our emotions becoming focused on ourselves, that's the moment to pause and see if we are missing something.

The "We" focus notices that the good and the bad that I experience touches other people. What you go through has already touched Yahweh's life before you ever existed. This is why we want to include Him in our moments. There are other folks around, even if you don't notice them. Focusing on the "we" of life begins when we are alone. "How am I going to be today." It does not matter what your plans or goals are; the state of being that matters. This is often a real challenge for me emotionally because I can put too much priority on my goals or plans only to sabotage them by not being in the right frame of mind.

When I look outside of myself and the little world I created for myself, I see many factors that can help or hinder me. Sometimes, the best way to help myself is to help someone else, especially when I don't want to. Other times, I have to take care of myself.

Balancing Me and We

You are essential, and so are the people around you. The best question is, "What will help the most right now?" You made plans and are ready to implement them. However, something unexpected has come up that may change all those plans. The question then becomes, "What will help the most right now?" Yep, it's the same question. As life keeps moving and changing, that one question will be a guiding principle.

Sometimes, you have to say the opposite of what you want. Other times, you must disappoint someone because you realize that something or someone else is more important. Each decision is a judgment call. The best judgment calls are the ones you believe are the right ones. You may still be correct, but it's better to do what you think is right and be wrong than to do what you feel is wrong and discover that you were right. If unsure, don't sabotage by picking what seems wrong because you need clarification, or it is the lesser of two evils. Go with what is the most right.

My grandfather told me once that when faced with two good decisions, "go with the hardest one." He also told me that he never regretted picking the most difficult one. Some of my best days have been when I did not accomplish what I set out to do but helped others instead. I've had some good days doing what I set out to do. It's the ebb and flow. In between are the days where I did not accomplish anything, either. Yes, I regret those.

Relationship Days

Some of my favorite days were when I worked on my relationships. Nothing can replace time spent with someone you value. It did not matter what happened; it was the time spent with that person that made it special. I had a great uncle who took me fishing as a teenager. It frustrated me so much that he could effortlessly catch fish while I struggled to return an empty hook. Now, I remember how nice it was that I spent time with him. It was a blessing. After mowing his yard, I would go inside and drink a cool beverage and chat with him about whatnot. On rare occasions, I drive by his old house, and it brings back fond memories.

The "It's okay" Moment

There was this moment after returning from training in another state, which I enjoyed that I felt let down and vulnerable. I was gone for a month and was having a good time. The home was somewhere that I was not enjoying. It was only a place to sleep. I also lost contact with people on a friendship level and felt very lonely. To make matters worse, I had to take a test that left me feeling drained and on the verge of despondency. I felt alone and empty. The next day, I went to the park to walk, pray, and read my Scriptures and another book. I began to take my mind off of my circumstances. The other was a Christian book whose topic was interesting but had nothing to do with my situation. When I was done, I felt re-energized. At that moment, I regained the feeling of "It's okay." My joy began to return, and so did my positive outlook. There was still a bit of emptiness as I faced several uphill challenges that would take time to work out, but it was okay. I wasn't where I wanted to be, far from it, but it was okay. I was heading in the right direction. Remember these words, *"Now faith is the substance of things hoped for, the evidence of things not seen."* Heb 11:1 NKJV.

I am still trying to figure out what I am working on today. Nor will I have it tomorrow. I will have it someday if I do not give up. That's what makes it okay. Since it is okay, I can focus on other things I need or should do. Those other things take my mind off of what I am missing, help me to feel accomplished, and move my life forward in other important ways. Now, I don't have to dwell on what is dragging me down. Since I am building myself back up, I can see how it will be okay.

Again, prayer time sets the stage for the Father to help make things okay. Notice that before it became okay, I had taken time to pray. As I walked the park, I let Him know what was on my mind and how it was making me feel. He worked it out to rearrange my thoughts and emotions. In this way, while nothing outwardly had changed, I had changed.

Identity

There is nothing more important than your identity. It is the thing that the enemy attacks first and last. Identity gets lost during times of emotional crisis. What was left of your identity was what helped you to survive. Now is the time to rebuild it and strengthen it.

When Adam and Eve were created, they were friends with Yahweh, face to face. The evil one challenged them in the area of their identity. He tempted them to be Yahweh's equals instead of friends. They learned too late that being friends was the greatest honor.

You were created to be yourself. Yet, from the time you were little, some people wanted to control what that was. It wasn't all bad. Others simply wanted what was best for you and worked to conform to society's norms. Most people in your life were just trying to help you, even though it was out of ignorance. They wanted you to be normal. Not that anyone can rightly define what "normal" is. You were supposed to fit in and live an "okay" life. Yahweh created you to stand out in your way – not weirdly or in an oddball sense. You have things about you that improve the lives of those around you. Maybe you are quirky or just see things from a different perspective.

I have read many stories from World War II. The ones that touch me are the ones from people who survived either the Prisoner of War camps or the Nazi concentration camps. The ones who typically survived were the ones who had a strong identity and self-worth to outlast the circumstances they found themselves in. Without a strong identity, a person's self-worth and goals crumble and fade under intense emotional pressure.

What happens after the pressure is relieved? Some people are left with no identity. The pressure became their new identity, and losing the pressure meant losing their new identity. Now, they are lost, which creates a new kind of pressure that the enemy exploits from within.

Regaining our identity is done with our Creator's help. He truly knows us and does not forget us. Starting there will prevent us from having a false identity implanted within us. First, Yahweh wants to be in a relationship with Him. Out of that relationship comes our true identity. He puts in us the desires that satisfy us. As we work on fulfilling those desires, we become the person we were meant to be. Second, we have to block out the noise that the enemy puts in our ears, both physical and spiritual. The enemy is always trying to take your identity away from you. Third, your identity is always tied to someone and something bigger than you. Of course, you know the Someone. Do you know what belongs to Him? From what is part of Him and His Kingdom comes your identity. If you have been reading Scripture, you know there is a difference between those who belong to Him and those who belong to the enemy. If you have not started reading Scripture, you will find your answers there and begin to understand who you are in Him.

Who you are is a combination of the talents you were born with, the skills you have picked up, the leading of the Spirit, and how you feel you can be the most useful. You have desires placed in you that, as you normalize, you feel them stirring back up, yet in a different way than before your emotional crisis. These stirrings direct you to be the person you ultimately want to be. It would be nice if identity were just a label we could place on ourselves and walk around with it. It is not a label. It is a way of living. Your purpose in life comes out of your identity. Once you choose your identity, you choose your path.

As you see your path in your mind, know that it will be there when you think you are going in a different direction than you thought the heavenly Father would take you. His detours take you straight to where you need to be after you go in a direction that would take longer or get you lost. Don't worry if you need a course correction. You cannot see everything and are doing the best you can. So let Him make adjustments, even the unexpected ones.

Your true self is something precious. As you embrace it, you will begin to relax in ways that you did not before and certainly not during your crisis. Relaxing allows you to see more since stress reduces your field of vision. The good news is that you are going to like who you are. There was a time when I did not think that was true. Now, strangely enough, I do. It's like a new life. Hope gives life to our identities. As our identities flourish, so do the people around us that the Father places in our lives to help us grow.

Letting Go

Letting Go is the last thing we do when we have truly begun to recover and live a new life. For me, it was 14 months after my plunge into the darkness of suicidal ideation. I had forgiven the people involved many, many times. and had even tried to just let it go. I could not seem to let it go. Then, one day, I had this peace come over me. I prayed to the Father, took a deep cleansing breath, and finally was able to let go. After that, I had a peace that transcended the circumstances.

It takes a willful decision to forgive and want the best for the ones who hurt you. It's a conscious decision to treat others how you would like to be treated if the situation were reversed. Why is it a good practice? Becomes sometimes, you can be the bad guy.

Letting go is a full, almost unconscious decision. It comes deep within after the willful, conscious decision. It is the understanding that you can let things simply be right or wrong. You don't have to fix it, deal with it, or manage it. You just make the ultimate choice to move on without the emotional baggage. It does not mean that some things won't need to be taken care of in the future. Things are different than the feelings you have about a persona. Those persons may have things that need to be dealt with. The difference is that your feelings towards them are clean and clear.

The ones who wounded you may never appreciate, care, or understand, but you do. When you release them and the hurt in one final act of healing, you become the person you were meant to be at the end of all of this.

Prayer

"Dear heavenly Father, I thank you for teaching me through all this hardship the things I needed to become the person You and I want me to be. I let all the hurt, anguish, pain, and ill will go. I forgive those who have wounded me. You have stood by me and have protected me through everything. I look to You for my hope, help, and healing. You are my Rock, my Fortress, my Mighty Defender. I love You. I want to honor You and to be more like You. You have forgiven everyone who asked, even those who once hated and hurt You. You love them despite every painful thing they have done to you. You do the same for the pain I cause You. I release them, the hurt, and the memories to You. I put them in your hands to take off and to handle. Please, take me and teach me to be Yours. I love You. In Yahushua's Name, amein."

Epilogue of Dealing with PTSD

I was almost done writing this book when I began to realize that I couldn't be the only person who went through serious suicidal ideation and came out the other side with at least some Post Traumatic Stress Disorder.

I had an episode of PTSD several decades ago when I had attended an all-night house fire as an EMT while working on an Indian reservation ambulance service. The details are quite gory. So, I will spare you some of the details. Suffice it to say that we were required to take the burned bodies out of the house, package them, and transport them to another home, as was their burial custom.

Later, when I went to church, I broke down crying. Thankfully, the pastor's father saw me and came to comfort me. For some 20 minutes, I could not stop. The tears just flowed down my face. I was so thankful for his help and comfort.

It took three months before I could smell grilled beef and not want to vomit. I hated driving by Burger King because that smell was the strongest. So, I found alternate routes just so I would not have to be confronted by the odor. My girlfriend's dad had a cookout one night. When I walked past the grill, I got a powerful whiff of the hamburgers. I ran to the bathroom and vomited.

Expect the Unexpected

Even today, I am on high alert if I have to talk to my ex-wife. The fight or flight mechanism kicks right in every time, which is a function of post-traumatic stress on my body because my mind remembers what happened and has made that situation a part of my body's defense mechanism.

The first time I saw her picture on social media, it was like being hit with a tazer and at the same time a stun grenade exploded. It was painful! Freaking unexpected! I never thought in my wildest dreams that this awful divorce would have left me with PTSD. With several of my recent jobs, I had dealt with a substantial number of angry outbursts and even violence. A few incidents required me to seek medical attention, and a few others left scars and bruises. None of which left me with PTSD. So, I figured that I was immune to post-traumatic stress. No! I was not even a little bit immune to it. The mind games that were played in my marriage were embedded deeply into my psyche. When they came out, it was explosive and physically painful. That's the power of the mind over the body, and it can be extreme.

I did not know that reaction was even possible. Especially since I had been practicing forgiveness. Well, forgiveness and healing from psychological trauma don't necessarily walk hand in hand. Sometimes, forgiveness must be practiced to be achieved at the deepest levels.

Corrie Ten Boom told a story about an incident in which she was confronted by the memories of her past in the Nazi Concentration Camps where she lost her sister. She was on tour promoting forgiveness. The talk occurred in Munich, Germany, only a couple of years after the war and her liberation from the camps.

After the talk was over, one of the former prison guards came up to her. This is how she recalled that moment, "But I remembered him and the leather crop swinging from his belt. It was the first time since my release that I had been face to face with one of my captors, and my blood seemed to freeze." Two years had gone by, but it was as if she was immediately returned to the horrors of the camp. That's PTSD in a nutshell.

The guard asked her for forgiveness. Although he did not remember her, he knew that he was in Ravensbruck at the same time she was. So, he humbled himself and asked for forgiveness. She said it was "the most difficult thing I had ever had to do." This is how she said it went, "And still I stood there with the coldness clutching my heart. But forgiveness is not an emotion – I knew that, too. Forgiveness is an act of the will, and the will can function regardless of the temperature of the heart.

'Jesus, help me!' I prayed silently. 'I can lift my hand. I can do that much. You supply the feeling.'

And so woodenly, mechanically, I thrust my hand into the one stretched out to me. And as I did, an incredible thing took place. The current started in my shoulder, raced down my arm, sprang into our joined hands. And then this healing warmth seemed to flood my whole being, bringing tears to my eyes.

'I forgive you brother!' I cried. 'With all my heart!'

For a long moment we grasped each other's hands, the former guard and the former prisoner. I had never known God's love so intensely as I did then." *Boom, Corrie ten, Brett Leveridge, Tonya May Avent, and Celeste McCauley. "Guideposts Classics: Corrie Ten Boom on Forgiveness." Guideposts, July 24, 2014. https://guideposts.org/positive-living/guideposts-classics-corrie-ten-boom-forgiveness/*

What an amazing story. I first heard it on the radio. Then I found it online. I wish I could say that when I went about forgiving my ex-wife, it was so healing, but it was the opposite. I worked for a long time to forgive. The PTSD episodes continued – not just months, but for years.

I am at the other end of the spectrum from Corrie Ten Boom. For me, forgiveness and PTSD ran counter to one another. However, time does heal all wounds if there is forgiveness. It took months for the painful PTSD reaction to subside. I had to say out loud many times, "I forgive."

I like what Corrie Ten Boom went on to say about forgiveness, "For I had to do it – I knew that. The message that God forgives has a prior condition: we forgive those who have injured us. 'If you do not forgive men their trespasses,' Jesus says, 'neither will your Father in heaven forgive your trespasses.'

I knew it not only as a commandment of God, but as a daily experience. Since the end of the war, I had had home in Holland for victims of Nazi Brutality.

Those who were able to forgive their former enemies were able also to return to the outside world and rebuild their lives, no matter what the physical scars. Those who nursed their bitterness remained invalids. It was as simple and as horrible as that."

They didn't have the term Post-Traumatic Stress Disorder back then, but people still experienced it. I believe that forgiveness is the only way to move past whatever brought you to the desire to end your life. It will help you move forward to what you want and what the heavenly Father wants for you.

There was a moment when I wished I had never met the woman, and I pondered what my life would have been like if I had been spared from the experience. Then, I realized that I would not be who I am today. Nor would I have the opportunities that I have today. Even the heartaches that I have with my sons as a result of the divorce would not exist because they would not exist. Nor would my grandchildren, who I hope to see someday. The pain of the divorce continues through the children. It serves to remind me of why I chose a better path, and why I need to fight for a better future.

Dealing with PTSD

I only want to give you what worked for me. I understand that someone else may say it in a way that's better for you. If what I say is not useful, please keep looking and moving forward.

What worked for me:
1.   Don't run from it.
2.   What happened is normal.
3.   Forgive until it is forgiven.
4.   Journal and move on.
5.   Plan for your future and work on it.
6.   Deal with the pain as it comes up.
7.   View it as a beneficial experience.

Don't Run from it

As you saw with Corrie Ten Boom, she wanted to run from it but quickly realized it would only hurt her more. Talking about it to someone you trust is extremely helpful, especially when you cannot speak to someone who hurt you.

I was never really able to talk to my ex-spouse because of the blame issues. However, over time, talking it out with others lessened the pain. I expect that one day, the PTSD reactions will be gone. I prayed many prayers about it, and I began to see the Father's hand working things out. Then, those requests turned into prayers of thanksgiving.

Yes, it hurts to deal with what happened. However, each time, it gets a little better. After a while, you can use it to help someone else, and it won't hurt as you talk about it the way you did before. I'm not saying that it will never stop hurting. It's like exercise; it gets easier the more you exercise.

What Happened is Normal

This was, and sometimes still is, a really hard one for me. First, I felt isolated and alone, so it seemed unique. Second, I liked feeling unique, but feeling unique was not helping me heal. Third, I felt betrayed that I had to go through it. Why did Yahweh allow it? This is a rather standard question.

We all like to feel special. When we are hurt, we no longer feel special. Sometimes, we get a chip on our shoulder and feel arrogant, afterward saying, "Nobody was hurt like I was." In reality, everybody has been hurt and betrayed. It's expected to be used, abused, and discarded. Sadly, more people have been badly wounded emotionally than have not. So, if you can admit that what you have experienced is part of the normal human condition, you become part of humanity rather than feeling like an outsider.

On the other hand, I believe one of the biggest reasons PTSD goes unhealed is the feeling of embarrassment and the isolation that it brings. Often, people cannot talk about it because they feel others won't understand. Some cannot understand, but some certainly do.

It can be very healthy to watch or read stories about people who were unjustly abused but turned their lives into something better, especially if you can internalize that concept and make it work for you. I remember the moment when I learned that I'm just normal, no better or worse than the next guy or gal. It was a friend at work who made me realize that. While it bruised my ego for a moment, it made me open up to the reality that pain and disappointment were normal and not something to be either ashamed of or arrogant about. That released a lot of tension. I was just normal, and normal is okay.

Forgive until it's Forgiven

I have had small moments in my life where I forgave someone, and it was an instant release—not to the point that Corrie Ten Boom experienced. However, I can understand what she was getting at and appreciate it.

My experience with my ex-wife required constant forgiving. Sometimes, it was because the PTSD somehow blocked my ability to feel like I had forgiven her. At other times, her current behavior brought back old memories and feelings. What I can say is that as time went on, her new behaviors did not affect me the same way as before. I'm not saying that I was not hurt or disappointed. What I am saying is that forgiving had become a habit, and I started to expect her behavior and emotionally prepare for it.

So, what lessened the PTSD was that I began to realize her behavior was the "new normal" and to plan on forgiving. I also realized that her behavior had been there all along, but it worsened over time and through different circumstances. Once I understood that she was just being average in her mind, then I could forget about confronting her behavior and letting it go. Then, as time passed, I could begin dealing with her based on reality instead of crushed fantasy.

Some people who hurt us honestly believe they are doing what is right, even if it is only in their own eyes. We often don't see how we contribute to that from their perspective. Sometimes, we are wrong and don't realize it for quite a while. Other times, the person hurting us literally cannot see the problem. For some reason, they cannot believe that they have injured us and genuinely think that we have wounded them.

Forgiveness spares us the continued pain of dealing with a perspective that we cannot understand or logically deal with. If we accept that we cannot change them but can only forgive them, we can heal regardless of what they do or don't do.

Journal and Move On

Even though I had received a certain level of healing from talking about my experiences, it wasn't until I journaled them that I had the biggest breakthrough. Maybe it was that I no longer had to remember them for the future. After all, it was written down somewhere for me to go back and review if I was concerned that I forgot something or was misremembering.

Because I didn't have to try to remember, I could move on, and that was very cathartic. It released a lot of anxiety. For me, it was a big emotional hurdle to get to the point of putting it on paper. Therefore, when I finally was ready to write it down, I was able to really deal with my thoughts and confront them head-on. After that, it wasn't so important to think about the past. It killed two birds with one stone.

Plan for your Future and Work on it

Thinking about the past often ruins the future. It's one thing to learn from the past and use those lessons. It's another to wallow in the past. I have had to learn not to do that. The only thing that works for me is to look at my future and decide what I want it to be. Naturally, it won't happen if I don't expend the energy to make it happen.

What do you want? What do you need to do to make it happen? This is where praying takes focus. Your heavenly Father knows what's best for you. He doesn't usually plop it down onto your lap. As you read His word and pray for His will, things begin to take shape. It's okay if you don't know what that looks like now.

The Father wants to be a part of our lives and our future. Therefore, we should take the time to pray and walk it out with Him. In this way, we are never alone. He has resources He wants to use that we know nothing about. So, putting your plans to work with Him opens up a whole new world.

The enemy is going to try to sabotage you. Occasionally, this helps us to focus. Why is the enemy trying to destroy what we are building? Usually, it's because it's terrible for them. The other problem that may frustrate us is that we need to be in the right place mentally or relationally. Therefore, praying, meditating, and seeking the Father's will help get us back on track. It is usually one of those two things.

Don't be surprised if one or more of your plans differ from the will of the Father. It happens to everybody. It's okay to adjust and see what the new plans are. Sometimes, it's simply a matter of seeing something the Father has for you, but you are out of focus. Try to refocus to see what is coming into view.

Deal with the Pain as it Comes up

I don't know about anyone else, but the pain of what made me initially want to commit suicide often comes back around. I hate the feeling of being vulnerable and weak. When I feel like someone else can control me and hurt me, I experience those awful feelings welling up. I wish it was like the time that I swore off committing suicide years ago. I'm not that person anymore. The feelings do come back these days. Sometimes, it's not my thoughts. So, I rebuke the demon, trying to replant it back in my head. Other times, it's my thoughts that I have to take captive.

The only thing that has helped me is simply taking it head on. In the first few months that my ex's picture was causing physical pain, I would deliberately look at the picture despite what would happen. After a while, the pain lessened. I would like to say that it was a predictable pattern. One day, after I had stopped seeing that picture, somehow, it popped back up again and caused a relapse of considerable pain. I was shocked initially but didn't let it get to me. It wasn't as bad as the first time, and I knew it was a fluke. The following year, I had very little pain when it reappeared. The repetition of dealing with the pain gave me emotional strength at the same time that it caused the pain to dissipate. That's your biggest key right there.

View it as a Beneficial Experience

Yep, that's easier said than done—until you start doing it. It can take a little bit of time to see the benefits. As you begin to see your first benefit, it becomes easier to see more of them. I won't lie to you. It can take more time than you think, even years, to see the benefits of your path. Don't be surprised if, a couple of years later, you're not a hundred percent sure of the reason you are on this path.

Here are a few benefits that I have found in the short run that you can expect to experience. First, you can be a better overall person than you were before. You may be blessing people in a way you don't yet see. Of course, you need to choose to be a better person. PTSD can grind you down to the point that you don't want to be the right person you know you can be. So it's a choice. Your power is in choosing. Next, you can use your experiences to help others, which can sometimes be very pleasant. This is a hard one. You can see how others are going down a bad path when they make negative choices. This can be sadly reassuring because you don't want to watch them suffer. It is a way for you to see that you are in a much better place and headed in the right direction. You can intervene and help them if they let you. Lastly, you become a stronger, more confident person by embracing the experience and learning from it. This means that when life gets hard again, you are much more prepared to deal with it than you were before. Someday, you may realize that you are dealing with a much harder problem than you had previously, but this time, you are succeeding because you learned the lessons of the past.

PTSD Reminds you that a New World is being Birthed in your Life

If you have ever seen a woman give birth or have done so yourself, you know that there is nothing easy about birthing a new life. Sometimes, I wonder what it is like for that new baby. I don't remember being born – and I am happy about that. It must be quite a shock to be born.

On the other side of a traumatic experience is a new life. No, it's not easy. What made it easier for me was embracing the new life and the unpleasant experiences it often brought. By facing them, I could move on faster. Dealing with my ex-wife was never pleasant, and occasionally, she made sure that it was not. However, I began to rebuild my emotional strength so that I could deal with what had to be done more appropriately and confidently, no matter how unpleasant it was. I also did not know when to admit I did not handle it appropriately.

The PTSD caused me to make a whole bunch of mistakes in leaving the relationship. As I began to take hold of my new life, I began to work to reverse the damage she did as she took advantage of my lack of confidence and focus on the long term.

As time passed, I got a new job that paid better and was substantially less stressful. I moved to a place where I had to learn how to deal with a less-than-ideal situation and make it work to my benefit. I had to learn how to deal with my two boys as the dust from the divorce began to settle.

Prayer

"Dear heavenly Father, thank you for helping me

to reach this season. I pray that you will continue to walk with me through the pain that came from the trauma that I endured. Teach me to use my suffering to help someone else recover and become strong. Restore to me what the enemy has taken away so that I can become the person you meant for me to be, and thank you for never letting me out of your sight. In Yahushua's name, amein."

A New Future

When I was growing up, the prophet Elijah was one of my favorite people in Scripture. He was a real firebrand. I loved his assertiveness and how we exuded such great confidence. Yet, he struggled at one time with wanting to live.

His story began when he went to confront the evil that King Ahab was doing in the kingdom of Israel. King Ahab brought in many pagan priests to lure his people away from worshiping Yahweh. At an appointed time, Yahweh used Elijah to confront both the king and the people of Israel to decide which deity they would serve. They agreed to a showdown.

For years, Israel was serving Ba'al and not Yahweh. What is essential to understand is Ba'al is the one we would consider to be the Devil. So, worshiping Ba'al was not an innocent mistake. It was embracing evil and death.

The king assembled hundreds of the priests of Ba'al, and Elijah stood alone for Yahweh. Two altars were constructed, and two bulls were cut up on the altars. For hours, the priests of Ba'al prayed, cried, and even cut themselves to get Ba'al to rain down fire and consume the sacrifice. At the time of the evening sacrifice in the Temple of Yahweh, Elijah had them prepare the bull. However, unlike the bull for Ba'al, it was drenched in water. Then, after praying, fire immediately fell from heaven, burning up the sacrifice and all of the water.

The victory was so great that Elijah executed all of the priests of Ba'al for their false worship. Even King Ahab sat down to eat the victory meal. However, when Queen Jezebel found out, she had a very different reaction than her husband. She threatened to kill Elijah, and that is when he left town. After Elijah stopped, he asked Yahweh to kill him because he saw no more value in his life. One moment, he was experiencing the thrill of victory. The next, he was running for his life. Today, we would say that Elijah was asking for assisted suicide.

What did Yahweh do? He gave His servant some food and water and then had him travel from Israel to Mt. Sinai in Saudi Arabia—the same mountain that Moshe took the Children of Israel to after leaving Egypt after the Passover meal. There, He talked to Elijah. While it was not an easy conversation, Elijah was a renewed man.

One of the problems Elijah faced was feeling alone, which was one of the reasons that he wanted to die. However, Yahweh told him that 7,000 other men had not bowed their knees in worship to Ba'al. After this, Elijah would be the force of encouragement. One of the people he encouraged was Elisha, who would be the one to take his place and continue his ministry. So, if he had died when he wanted to, he would have missed out on some of the most history-changing elements in his story, including having his ministry continue after he was gone. One thing that vindicated him was that he lived to see the deaths of his enemies. What can we say? There is a lot of history to be made in living.

Now, Elijah's story does not end there. One of the most surprising things is that the man who asked Yahweh to kill him never died. He was taken up into heaven in a whirlwind, alive. So, how did Elijah achieve this? Fundamentally, Elijah made Yahweh his whole life. There came a point when he simply could not go along in life with Yahweh being just his spiritual leader. Yahweh became his only option.

What does this have to do with us? Great question! We are living in a time similar to Elijah's. Things are getting worse and getting weird. Suicide rates are increasing. One obvious fact is that in times of great darkness, the smallest light can shine brightly. There is hope for those who live because Yahweh can care for us as He cared for Elijah. Yahweh rewards those who are faithful. Interestingly, one of the best rewards is that those who are faithful during the Greatest Tribulation in mankind's history will be rescued from it and never die, just like Elijah.

The Apostle Paul put it this way, *"According to my earnest expectation and hope that in nothing I shall be ashamed, but with all boldness, as always, so now also Christ will be magnified in my body, whether by life or by death. For to me, to live is Christ, and to die is gain. But if I live on in the flesh, this will mean fruit from my labor; yet what I shall choose I cannot tell. For I am hard-pressed between the two, having a desire to depart and be with Christ, which is far better. Nevertheless to remain in the flesh is more needful for you."* – Phil 1:20-24 NKJV.

Remaining alive to help others, especially in times of darkness, is the greatest ministry we can have in this life. That is why Paul chose to live. In the end, he died a martyr's death, but he will be resurrected when Messiah returns. So, he will live again, and he will have the victor's crown of faithfulness. Our lives can be the blessing others desperately need by choosing to live. Both Elijah and Paul went on to be the blessing that others needed.

One of the exciting things about this era is that we may very well be the ones chosen to never die if we make the choice to live for Him. Or we may be asked to remain faithful no matter what. The blessing is the abundant reward for faithfulness to Him. As the Word says, *"But without faith it is impossible to please Him, for he who comes to God must believe that He is and that He is a rewarder of those who diligently seek Him."* – Heb 11:6 NKJV—the blessings of being one of the ones who overcome.

The enemy is trying to sabotage us in so many different ways, especially in these peculiar days. I encourage you to overcome the tactics of chaos. In the book of Revelation, eight blessings are given to those who overcome the enemy's different ways to defeat us. If you overcome any of those things, you are promised one or more of Yahushua's incredible blessings to His faithful ones.

1. To eat of the Tree of Life in the paradise of Yahweh.
2. Never be hurt by the second death.
3. Be given the hidden manna and a white stone with a new name.
4. Be given the authority over the nations.
5. Given a white garment, never will your name be erased from the Book of Life, and your name be confessed before the Father and the angels.
6. Be made a pillar in the sanctuary of the Mighty One.
7. To sit with Yahushua on His throne.
8. He will always be your Mighty One, and you will be His child.

Nothing that death has is better than any of these things. In death, there is emptiness. Abundance comes from accepting life and the challenges that come with it. It is in the abundance that we know that we have succeeded. After Elijah chose to live once again for Yahweh, he saw many victories. Elijah embraced the courage to live, and when you do, you will one day be honored before the throne of Yahweh. Make Yahweh your life.

Benediction

I wrote this book to put my mind back together, and I hope my perspective will be helpful. I am a survivor, and this is a survivor's perspective. It is not a mental health expert's opinion or years of experience with patients. However, it is a way for me to grow while trying to be a blessing to others who are dealing with similar issues. I hope it's like one friend helping another friend. I chose life which has allowed me to pursue more hopes and dreams.

I pray you find the courage to pursue your hopes and dreams. May you lovingly grab hold of the heavenly Father's Hand and walk down a new road, able to handle new challenges, no matter how difficult or frightening, because lasting joy is on the other side. Here's to a new life!

www.ingramcontent.com/pod-product-compliance
Lightning Source LLC
Chambersburg PA
CBHW052116030426
42335CB00025B/3014